British and Irish Mythology

BRITISH AND IRISH MYTHOLOGY

An Encyclopedia of Myth and Legend

Caitlín and John Matthews

Illustrated by Chesca Potter

DIAMOND
BOOKS

This edition published 1995 by
Diamond Books
77–85 Fulham Palace Road
Hammersmith, London W6 8JB

First published by The Aquarian Press as
The Aquarian Guide to British and Irish Mythology 1988

ISBN 0 261 66651 7

Printed in Great Britain

Contents

'I have made a heap of all that I have found....'
Nennius, *History of the British*

'Thou Genius of the place (this most renowned Ile)
Which livedst long before the All-earth-drowning Flood,
Whilst yet the world did swarme with her Gigantick brood;
Go thou before me still thy circling shores about,
And in this wandring Maze helpe to conducte me out.'
Michael Drayton, *Polyolbion*

'Britain, the best of islands, is situated in the Western Ocean between France and Ireland. (It) is inhabited by five races of people, the Norman-French, the Britons, the Saxons, the Picts and the Scots.'
Geoffrey of Monmouth, *The History of the Kings of Britain*

Dedication

To the ancestors—especially our parents:
Muriel and Frank and Fred and Olive

Introduction

When the Monk Nennius compiled his British *History* in the ninth century from diverse literary and oral sources, he said that he had 'made a heap' of all he could find. From such a compost heap comes our own Guide to British and Irish Mythology composed of layers of diverse matter in various stages of disintegration and reformation. As every gardener will tell you, there is nothing like good compost for a healthy garden. As mythographers, we would assert that there is nothing like a good myth to keep our consciousness thriving imaginatively.

The people, gods and heroes of this book have all made their own individual contribution to the mythic consciousness of the British Isles. Today we make our own mythologies, but it remains for our descendants to decide whether they shall pass into popular consciousness. In this age of media culture and affordable paperbacks, it is hard to recall a time when the memory and oral tradition were the only methods of recording and retrieving. Should there come a time, however, when computer records could not be consulted or were lost, or when there were no more forests to cut down in order to print books, we might well find ourselves in such a situation once again. Would our memories or common consciousness be able to cope?

Indeed, Nennius says that he had to put together his own chronicle of Britain's history and arcane lore because he felt the oral tradition was insufficiently effective for future transmission to later generations. We must admit that some of the entries in our own mythical encyclopaedia could not have been printed here, had they not been recorded at some point by zealous chroniclers and story-tellers. Those that were recorded had, in many cases, been heavily embroidered or pied with other stories; but so does the strata of myth become established.

Clearly any mythical encyclopaedia can never be considered all inclusive. Scope and criteria will always remain the eclectic decision of the compilers. Thus in order to keep this volume to a manageable size, we have concentrated on what we consider to be the most central myths which, with few exceptions, are the earliest.

In each instance we asked ourselves the question: 'shall these bones live?' Some myths are so fragmentarily preserved or utterly lost — but for their protagonists' names — it might be asked, 'why bother?' These pathetic shards are often the 'missing link' which show the continuity of a tradition and where such characters appear crucial we have included them.

Myth is more than an outpost of folk-lorists. It is the living centre where the heart of the people beats strongest, giving a sense of identity and a will to achieve or overcome obstacles. This is not so clear to us now because we have substituted other, weaker myths, derived from the evanescent media culture. Everyone needs myth because it nourishes the psyche. In later years, we have become content with the ready-packaged kind rather than home-produce. In saying this we are not being racially chauvinist. The British Isles owes its peoples and culture to a long succession of visitors who have settled down, adding their own special thread to the tapestry. Without fresh views on the world, the British Isles would not have survived as a cultural entity. But our mythic tradition must go on being endlessly enriched, not stultified.

Singers and story-tellers are needed, but so are avid listeners and readers. We hope that you will go away and read the great mythic stories, making them your own by recreating them endlessly in your imagination. There is no Ministry for Mythic Consciousness to keep our mythology alive. It is down to you to make it and to tell it to your children, that they might tell it to theirs.

We understand, however, that not everyone is willing or able to read the original texts, even in translation. For those who like their stories in more soluble form, we have included a reading-list composed of retellings by good authors at the back of the book. The general bibliography gives source texts, commentaries and background to British Mythology.

We hope that you will find the characters you are looking for in this book. As with all reference books, there is always something left out and we are conscious that one volume hardly suffices to cover such a wide subject. We hope most of all that these myths will not remain static in your imagination and that you will find the means to utilize them. Those of you who prefer your myths as living beliefs are referred to our *The Western Way* volumes 1 and 2 (Arkana 1985, 1986) for methods of practical working with myths. Go on reading, telling or singing the stories, for you and you alone are their continuance.

Caitlín and John Matthews
Candlemas 1987

Categorization of Names and Peoples

Who are our ancestors? Mythically, the Britons descend from Brutus who sailed from Troy to found his Troia Nova in Britain. The Irish descend, mythically, from Noah, from the Kings of Spain, Greece and Egypt. Atlantis is supposed to have cast up its survivors on our shores. Historians tell of invading hordes from Europe and Asia, each distinguished by the nature of its metal, pottery or artifacts. The founders of Western Scotland were really Irish Gaels; the Welsh were really the British and were only called 'wealas' or foreigner by the incoming Saxons. The Welsh, in order to distinguish themselves, called themselves Cymru. The Bretons were British. And who shall say who the English were? Strip off the layers and you find the mythic wallpaper of a former people. As with any house, you changed what you didn't like and kept the features which you did. The gods of one people became the devils or faery-kind of the next one. A name which once inspired awe and reverence became an object of fear or mockery.

As successive waves of influence have dashed against our shores, so has the existing coastline of the mythic dimension been modified and moulded. Yet the persistent retention of certain characters, archetypes and themes is remarkable, revealing the true nature of

British myth. Indigenous features, like our weather (which the Irish call 'soft' but which tourists find plain wet), form the prevailing climate of our belief. Sleeping kings who will come again, hags who become gift-bestowing maidens, wild men with staves and otherworld women with cups, are all part of our composite tradition. Whatever gods and beliefs have been brought to Britain, they have a way of settling in so that the sharp definition of their origins is gradually blunted until it blends into the ambience of the new homeland.

Such a general observation is all very well, but in acknowledgement of the fact that consulters of an encyclopaedia of this kind need frames of reference, definitions and select pigeon holes; the people, gods, heroes and traditions which make up this book are presented within a general alphabetical framework, with further categorization according to their origins. To have done justice to each entry by defining it according to its contents would have been a time-consuming exercise for us and an annoying one for the reader.

Each entry appears with its name's usual and variant spellings and is followed by a code-letter which designates its category. For example:

Perceval/Peredur/Perlesvaus/Parzival (A)

In this instance the character is defined as *Arthurian*. The key to this categorization is on p.16. There follows a breakdown of any story or mythos attached to that entry and relevant parallel stories. Characters which are mentioned in that entry appearing in their own right are italicized.

The categories and our reasons for defining them are as follows:

Arthurian It is not for nothing that the stories surrounding King Arthur are known as 'The Matter of Britain'. In this vast collection of material, oral tradition and literary exposition meet and intermingle to such a degree that it has proved impossible to be dogmatic about our criteria. We have included the earliest Welsh textual evidence as well as the later literary romance of Malory's 'Le Morte d'Arthur', and also the so-called 'Vulgate Cycle' of Arthurian myths, since both draw upon an older oral tradition. We have generally excluded the European contributions to 'The Matter of Britain', with the exception of mentioning some of the characters of Wolfram von Eschenbach's *Parzival*, in which such key native characters as *Cundrie* and *Anfortas* appear. Certain places, such as *Camelot* and *Sarras* gain entry here, because they typify the mythic landscape of Arthurian Britain. Famous objects, such as the *Grail*, *Excalibur*, and the *Round Table* are included. Minor objects and places which have their existence only in literary romances have been excluded. In short, we have tried to strike a balance between tradition and literature and to provide information of a kind that will be required by the questing reader.

Birds, Beasts and Fish We offer no apology for including animals in our criteria. Too often the helping animals, the totems spirits whose assistance was sought by the far ancestors of our race, have been excluded. However, they too are part of our deep mythology and, in many instances, have retained spiritual qualities which are still attested to in folklore today. Many archetypical characters, such as *Taliesin* or *Tuan mac Carill* actually employ animal guises, either as shape-shifters or as suitable forms in which to prolong their corporeal existence. Not every animal is mentioned here, only those who play a greater part in the mythology of these islands.

Celtic Some entries cannot be classified as either Welsh, Irish or Scottish, since they partake of one or all of these categories. Where this is so, as in the case of the *Mothers,* we have given in and called them Celtic as a blanket term. This is with the reservation that what we now term Celtic might well include earlier and uncategorizable native traits.

Greek Well, we did say that Brutus had fled from Troy to bring our ancestors home to Britain! A very few Greek characters have strayed in because of their associations with Britain. *Cronos* is chief among them, with *Apollo*: both were believed by the Greeks to have a special place in the islands which were believed to be at the back of the 'North Wind', in Hyperborea, of which Britain was considered to be part.

Irish Since Ireland never suffered major interference in its traditions, this category needs little explanation. However, it remains to be said, that while there is much extant material available to the non-Irish-speaking reader, there is a wealth of texts as yet untranslated awaiting the attention of early and middle Irish scholars, quite apart from a vast oral tradition which is in the last stages of its virility. It is hoped that those presently holding posts at the various seats of Celtic scholarship will extend their research and help open up this fascinating field to a wider readership. We have, in the main, stuck to the major mythological cycles of the Books of Invasions, *Fionn mac Cumhail* and *CuChulainn*, and the Cycles of the Kings — although the latter is only touched upon here.

Legendary Legendary kings, such as those appearing in Geoffrey of Monmouth's 'History of the British Kings', heroes and otherwordly beings make up this rag-bag category which combines ancient archetypes with strays from folklore and antique oral tradition. Some of the entries, e.g. *Black Annis*, belie the earliest neolithic strata of our mythic consciousness, while others like *Lear* also appear in their proto-Celtic forms.

Norse The presence of the Saxons has given us the name 'English', a term which we decided against in our categorization. The gods of the many Scandinavian visitors to our shores played no negligible part in our mythic history. Mythological scholarship runs in phases and at the turn of the century it was the turn of Celtic gods to come to the conscious attention of readers, ousting the long focus on the Northern and Germanic mythos. The tide is probably about to turn again. We have included only the major deities of the Norse pantheons and the heroes who were part of their tradition.

Roman and Romano-British The Roman presence in Britain was of only a few centuries' duration, but it left a lasting mark on our landscape and our consciousness. We have included Roman deities who have taken on a new existence of their own, like *Mars* who incorporated a good few local gods. The Romans had a habit (a very wise and polite one) of propitiating the local deity by setting up dedications to the *genius locus* and naming it after the nearest Roman deity. However, some gods precluded this practice, either because the locals protested too much, or because the Romans were themselves overwhelmed by the properties and functions of that god, and the name remained. A few hybrids grew up and it is not uncommon to find a Roman god with a Celtic consort, as with *Mercury* and *Rosmerta*. We have included the main Romano-British gods, noting that some may have been colonial imports from Gaul or other parts of Europe, as part of the bag and baggage of Roman occupation.

Scottish Like Wales, Scotland is a matter of shifting borders. Apart from the Highland fastnesses and the Western Isles which have their own Gaelic identity, we can trace Scandinavian, Cumbric and Northumbrian threads which incorporate the lost Pictish setts of mythology. A strong oral tradition has, as in Ireland, preserved many distinct ancient features.

Saints We have included a very select scattering of saints. We have concentrated on those who are national patrons like Saint Patrick and Saint George, or on those whose mythos bears on an already existing pagan tradition. Saints rapidly filled the vacuum left by the former gods of these islands, assimilating their legends and performing similar functions of help and guidance. The few we have included testify to an ongoing tradition.

Welsh As we already said, the Welsh call themselves Cymru. It is only other people who call them Welsh, however, that title seems to have stuck and we hope that they will not mind too much, in the secure knowledge that they are 'the real' British. Again, we have concentrated on the major sources such as the *Mabinogion* and the Triads for our entries. As with the Irish entries, there are woefully few translations of traditional stories for the non-Welsh speaker. We should bear in mind that for both Irish and Welsh speakers their language is the vehicle of their mythic consciousness: when Welsh and Gaelic disintegrate as living languages — and we hope that day may never come — it is in translation that their myths will live on.

Other Entries Some entries appear without categories because they represent historic people to whom myths have become attached or to whom feats of great heroism are attributed. *Charles I* is an odd man out since he is unofficially a saint as well as a king; less difficult to understand are *Hereward the Wake* and *William Wallace* — liberators with a purpose who slipped into legend.

User's Key

(A) = Arthurian   (I) = Irish   (RB) = Romano-British
(B) = Birds, Beasts   (L) = Legendary   (S) = Scottish
  and Fish
(C) = Celtic   (N) = Norse   (ST) = Saint
(G) = Greek   (R) = Roman   (W) = Welsh

Italicized names have their own entries.

The figures in square brackets at the end of an entry — e.g. [17,80] — refer to the numerated bibliography at the back of the book.

A

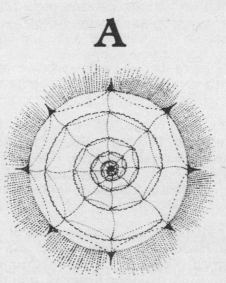

Arianrhod's Wheel

Abaris (G) Greek tradition makes Abaris a priest and servant of *Hyperborean Apollo*. He rode on a golden arrow as Apollo's messenger and visited Pythagoras, who received and initiated him. It is possible that he represents a holy man or druid from Britain. [57]

Accalon of Gaul (A) The champion and lover of *Morgan le Fay*, with whom he conspired to overcome *Arthur* by stealing the sword Excalibur which rendered it user immune to wounds. *Merlin* aided Arthur in his combat against Accalon and he was overcome. [20]

Adam Bell (L) One of three English outlaws famed for their skills in archery. When one, *William of Cloudesley*, was about to be hanged, Adam and *Clim of Clough* rescued him and went on to London to secure a pardon from the king, by skilfully shooting at an archery contest. All three were made free men.

Adder (B) As the only poisonous snake in the British Isles the adder has a reputation for wisdom and sly cunning. The amulets said to have been carried by the druids, 'gloine nathair' (the glass of the serpent), were really adder stones. It was an adder which caused the Battle of *Camlan*; while the armies of *Mordred* and *Arthur* were drawn up during a parley in which the battle might have been averted, an adder darted out from the scrub, so startling one of Arthur's men that he drew his sword to slay it. Taking the flash of his sword as an instance of Arthur's treachery, Mordred's army attacked. In the Highlands, the adder or serpent is supposed to represent the *Cailleach*'s power, which *Brigit* defeats with her lamb. (See *Samhain* and *Oimelc*.) [20, 183, 185]

Aed mac Lir (I) Son of *Aobh*. He was turned into a *swan* by his stepmother, *Aoife*.

Aegir Hler (N) God of the Sea, in its more benign aspect, unlike his wife, *Ran*, with whom he lived in a hall beneath the waves near the island of Hlesay.

Aes Sidhe (I) The Hosts of the *Sidhe* or Hollow Hills. The inhabitants of the Otherworld. They were thought to ride out on the eves of the four great fire festivals: *Samhain* (31 October), *Oimelc* (31 January), *Beltaine* (30 April), and *Lughnasadh* (31 July), when they had communion with earthly folk. Yeats wrote of them as 'The Hosts of the Air'. (See *Daoine Sidhe*.) [55]

Aesir (N) The gods of *Asgard*, lead by *Odin* and his sons *Thor*, *Balder*, *Tyr*, *Vali*, *Hoder*, *Bregi*, *Hermod*, *Vili* and *Ve* together with their wives *Frigga*, *Sif*, *Nanna*, *Iduna*. Also of their number was *Loki*, the troublemaker. They ruled the heavens from the dawn of time to *Ragnarok*, the ending of all things, and were in perpetual war with the *Frost Giants*. They met every day under the great world tree, *Yggdrasil*, to discuss matters relating to themselves and to mankind. They may originally have been a community of warrior gods, who gradually assumed a position of greater importance and finally 'took over' heaven. [1, 53]

Afagddu (W) See *Morfran*.

Afanc (W) A primeval monster which dwelt in the Llyn yr Afanc on the River Conwy in North Wales. It was sometimes thought to be in the shape of a beaver and dragged people into the depths of the lake. It was eventually hauled from the lake by oxen, after having been lured to sleep in a maiden's bosom. [28]

Aglovale (A) Son of King *Pellinore*. He was accidentally killed by *Lancelot* when he rescued *Guinevere* from the stake. [129]

Agravaine (A) *Round Table* Knight. He was the brother of *Gawain*, *Gaheris* and *Gareth*. Son of King *Lot* of Orkney and *Morgause*. His one moment of fame came when he plotted with *Mordred* to unmask the adultery of *Guinevere* and *Lancelot*, by whom he was slain when he attempted to arraign the queen in her chamber. [20]

Agretes (A) In the 'Grand Saint Greal', a thirteenth-century Arthurian romance, Agretes is described as the King of *Camelot* in a time long before *Arthur*. As a pagan he persecuted Josephus, son of *Joseph of Arimathea* and guardian of the *Grail*, and was punished by madness and death.

Aguigrenons (A) According to various *Grail* romances Aguigrenons was the General of King Clamadex, an evil monarch who entrapped many *Grail Knights*. *Perceval* finally overcame Aguigrenons when he defended the maiden *Blanchfleur*, and eventually sent both he and his master to *Arthur*'s court.

Aidan (ST) (d.651) Monk of Iona and Bishop of Lindisfarne. He was an Irishman who came to England and helped *Oswald* in the evangelization of Northumbria. He was on Inner Farne when he saw the burning of the royal castle of Bamburgh by pagan King Penda. Aidan prayed for the wind to change and it did so. His spiritual successor was *Cuthbert* who saw Aidan's glorious ascent to heaven. His symbol is the torch and his feast-day is 31 August.

Aideen (I) Wife of *Fionn mac Cumhail*'s grandson *Oscar*. She died of grief when he fell at the battle of Gabhra, and was buried on Ben Edar in Howth.

Ailill mac Matach (I) King of Connacht, husband of Medb, (see *Maeve*). He owned a great *bull* Finnbennach (Whitehorn), causing his wife to be jealous and covert the Donn Cuailuge (Brown One), a bull owned by an Ulsterman. This precipitated the great cattle-raid in which both Ulster and Connacht came to blows. Ailill was no match for his wife, who took her lovers indiscriminately, but he was responsible for the death of one of them — *Fergus mac Roigh*. Ailill himself was slain by *Conall Cernach* at the instigation of a jealous Medb after she found him lying with a maiden on May Day. [27, 99]

Aine (I) A goddess who seems to have functioned as a type of *Sovereignty* in south west Ireland. She gave her name to a *sidhe* dwelling in Munster, Cnoc Aine. She is variously described as the wife or daughter of *Manannan mac Lir*.

Later folk tradition tells of Gearoid Iarla (Earl Gerald of Desmond, 1338–98) who encountered Aine bathing in a river and raped her. The first earl of Desmond was called 'Aine's king' and Gerald himself 'the son of fair Aine's knight'. Gerald was said to have disappeared in the form of a goose, after a lifetime building up his reputation as a magician. This legend shows how active the myth of Sovereignty was persisting right into the medieval era. [90, 99]

Ainle (I) Brother of *Naoisi*, lover of *Deirdriu*.

Aisling (I) The word means dream or vision and is, in modern Irish, a woman's name, but in the many Irish tales bearing this title, the dreamer experiences a vision of a *speir-bhean* or vision-woman whose beauty leads him into closer communion with the Otherworld. A great many poets of the eighteenth century wrote Aisling poems, in which a fair woman is found wandering in poverty and distress. She represents the land of Ireland itself, oppressed under the English yoke. [186]

Alain le Gros (A) The father of *Perceval*, according to various texts. In one story he fed a multitude from a single fish and was afterwards known as the *Fisher King*. He also built the castle of *Corbenic* to house the *Hallows* of the *Grail*.

Alban (ST) Proto-martyr of Britain. He was a soldier and a pagan who sheltered a priest during one of the numerous persecutions of the Christians. Alban was himself converted to the faith and, dressed in the priest's garments to help him escape, was himself arrested and charged. He was executed on Holmhurst Hill where the great Abbey of St Albans was later built. He probably lived in the third century and was martyred at Verulamium, now St Albans. His feast day is 22 June.

Albanactus (L) The third son of *Brutus* after whom Albany or Scotland is named. [9]

Albion (L) The name of Britain before *Brutus* landed from *Troy*. William Blake personified Albion as a giant, associating him with *Cronos*, in his poetical and artistic works. [9, 39]

Aleine (A) *Gawain*'s niece. In the 'Didot Perceval' she sent *Perceval* a suit of red armour and persuaded him to take part in a tournament at *Arthur*'s court from which he had hitherto refrained. Thus disguised he carried all before him and won a place at the *Round Table*. [26]

Alfar (N) The original elves, later subsumed within native British Faery-lore. They were divided into two groups: the *Lios Alfar* or Light Elves, and the *Svart Alfar* or Dark Elves. The former lived in *Alfhelm* and were ruled over by *Frey*. The latter lived in an underground kingdom and were said by some to be ruled over by *Wayland the Smith*. They were confused with the Dwarves. J. R. R. Tolkien created a whole sub-mythology for them, in which the Lios Alfar were the servants of the Creator. His notion of the elves combined the Norse Alfar with the inhabitants of the Celtic *Blessed Islands* or the *Daoine Sidhe*. [53]

Alfasem (A) King of Terre Foraine and one of the *Wounded Kings*. After being baptised by *Alain le Gros* he attempted to look into the

Grail and was struck down for his temerity. He is healed when the Grail is achieved.

Alfhelm (N) The area of *Asgard* inhabited by the *Lios Alfar*, the elves of light, ruled over by *Frey*.

Alfred the Great (849-900) King of Wessex. He repulsed the Danes. It was while hiding in the marshes of Somerset on the Isle of Athelney that he was supposed to have burnt the cakes. He also had a vision of the Virgin at whose feet he cast a jewel as an offering. In 1693 such a jewel was found, inscribed 'Alfred had me made.' (This is now housed at the Ashmolean Museum, Oxford.)

Alfred codified laws, established the first real navy and was the translator of Boethius' 'Consolations of Philosophy'. He and *Arthur* are the two heroes who bracket that period called, by historians, the Dark Ages. Their two careers were concerned with the defence of Britain in battle and its civilization by means of the gentle arts.

Alice la Beale Pilgrim (A) Daughter of Ansirus le Pilgrim, one of *Lancelot*'s many cousins. She helped *Alisander le Orphelin* escape from the castle of *Morgan le Fay* and afterwards married him. She always kept her face veiled, suggesting she was of more than mortal beauty. It was when she was unveiled that Alisander fell in love with her.

Alisander le Orphelin (A) A knight who set out to avenge the murder of his father by King *Mark* of Cornwall, and who encountered many adventures upon the way. He was noticed at a tournament by *Morgan le Fay* who healed his wounds in order to make him her lover. He refused her and married *Alice la Beale Pilgrim*. He never reached *Camelot* and was numbered among Mark's knights.

Amatheon (W) Son of *Don*. He has passed out of most existing legends and stories, remaining only within 'Culhwch and Olwen', where he is described as a wild husbandman, and in the poem attributed to *Taliesin*, the 'Cad Goddeu', where he fights with his brother, *Gwydion*, against the *Arawn*, king of *Annwn*. The modern Welsh for farmer is still 'amaethwr', but we can only speculate as to the original nature of Amaethon, who may indeed have fulfilled the function of a patron of agriculture. [18, 28, 58]

Amangons (A) A cruel and avaricious king who lived before the times of *Arthur*, but whose actions determined much of the later quest for the *Grail*. Together with his followers, he raped the damsels of the wells and stole their golden cups. In Arthur's time, the descendants of these damsels and knights, lived deep in the forest. Behind this story is a powerful myth of otherworldly women, representing the *Sovereignty* of the land, who guard the *Hallows* of

Britain but whose guardianship is eroded and usurped, causing the *Wasteland*. Only the finding of the Grail can heal the land. [83]

Ambrosius (A) King of Britain, brother of *Uther Pendragon*. He spent his boyhood abroad after being deposed by *Vortigern*, but returned with Uther and regained his throne. According to historical evidence he led the British opposition against the Saxons and helped establish a foundation upon which *Arthur* was able to build. He is called The Last of the Romans. [72, 36]

Amergin (I) Son of *Miled*. He was the judge and poet of his people, whose great self-pronouncements echo those of *Taliesin*. He enabled his people to enter Ireland by successfully encountering the goddesses of *Sovereignty* — *Banba*, *Fodla* and *Eriu* — and promising to name the island after each of them. The *Tuatha de Danaan* asked him to judge between his people and themselves, but Amergin helped the sons of Miled to claim Ireland as their own. [15, 5, 99]

Aminadap (A) One of the line of *Grail Kings* alluded to in the 'Quest del Saint Graal'.

Amr/Anir (A) One of the sons of *Arthur*, of whom nothing is known but that he was apparently slain by his own father. His grave, Licat Amir, lay in Wales and was said never to measure the same length on any two nights. [28]

Andraste (C) Icenian warrior goddess of Victory, propitiated by *Boudicca* in her campaigns against the Romans. She was worshipped in a sacred grove. Boudicca released a *hare* as part of the rite of propitiation. [187]

Andred (A) *Tristan*'s cousin, who plotted his death or discredit, constantly spying on his assignations with *Isolt* and reporting them to King *Mark*. In some versions he is credited with the murder of Tristan, but is himself slain by Bellangere le Beuse, together with all those who had plotted Tristan's death. [20]

Andrew (ST) The patron of Scotland. Brother of Simon Peter, and fisherman of Capernaum. He became an apostle and tradition says he was martyred in Achaia by being crucified on a decussated or saltire cross. He was said to have given the Pictish army a vision of this cross at the battle of Athelstoneford between King Angus of the Picts and King Athelstan of the Angles. However, it is fairly clear that Andrew was foisted upon Scotland as its patron when the old Celtic and Culdee centres of Dunkeld and Abernethy were superseded by the new bishopric of St Andrew's. His feast-day is 30 November.

Anfortas (A) The *Grail King* in Wolfram von Eschenbach's 'Parzival', and Wagner's opera of the same name. [30]

Angharad (A) Loved by *Peredur* in the Welsh romance of the *Grail*.
Her full name is Angharad Law Eurawc, which means Angharad
Golden Hand. Peredur swore to love no other or to speak to any
man until she returned his feelings. She may possibly be a much
older Celtic deity, who like so many of her kind has dwindled to
a minor role in Arthurian romance. (See *Perceval*.) [18, 186]

Angrboda (N) The giantess upon whom *Loki* fathered several monstrous children, including *Hel*, *Fenris* and the *Midgard Serpent*.

Angus mac Og/Aengus/Oengus (I) God of youth. Son of *Dagda*
and *Boann*. He was called Mac Og (or the Young Son) after his
mother's words, 'Young is the son who was begotten at break of
day and born betwixt it and evening', referring to his magical conception and gestation. He was fostered by *Midir*.
    An eighth-century text, 'Aislinge Oenguso' (The Dream of Angus),
tells how he was visited by an otherworldly maiden, *Caer Ibormeith*,
in his sleep and conceived such a love for her that he fell ill until
he found her, with the help of *Bodb*. She was in the form of a *swan*
one year and assumed human shape the next. He found her at Loch
Bel Dracon at *Samhain*, together with 149 other girls all in swan-
form, with silver chains between each pair. Angus also assumed the
form of a swan, and together they circled the lake three times, singing sleep-music so profoundly moving, that everyone in the vicinity
fell asleep for three days and nights. They returned to his otherworldly palace, Bruig na Boinne (New Grange, Meath). W. B. Yeats'
poem 'The Song of Wandering Aengus' is a retelling of this
event.
    Angus, because of his magical birth, had power over time. When
the mounds of the *Sidhe* were being distributed between the *Tuatha
de Danann*, Angus arrived late and demanded to spend a day and
night in the dwelling of the Dagda. This was granted, but on the
following day when he was asked to leave, Angus said, 'It is clear
that night and day are the whole world, and it is that which has
been given to me.' Variants state that Angus was given the sidi of
Bruig na Boinne in place of his mother's husband, *Elcmar*. He was
the foster-father of *Diarmuid*. [19, 42]

Angwish/Agwisance (A) King of Ireland and father of *Iseult of
Ireland*. He seems to have fought against *Arthur* on the side of the
rebel Kings at the beginning of Arthur's reign. He later became a
companion of the *Round Table*. *Mark* of Cornwall owed him
allegiance and it was on account of *Tristan*'s coming to dispute this,
at which time he also killed Anguish's brother the *Morholt*, that
Tristan first saw Iseult. [20]

Anluan (I) One of the warriors of Connacht who accompanied
Queen *Maeve* on the famous cattle raid. He was subsequently slain

by Connall and his head displayed to his brother Cet during an exchange of boasts.

Anna (A) The sister of *Arthur*, according to Geoffrey of Monmouth. [9, 28]

Annowre (A) A sorceress of the Perilous Forest who desired *Arthur*. She succeeded in enticing him into the forest, but when he refused her she plotted his death, inviting various knights to kill him. *Nimue*, hearing of this, brought *Tristan* to the place where Arthur was held captive, just in time to kill two knights who had beaten him. The King himself slew Annowre, who had tried to steal *Excalibur*. The whole story may well be a variant of *Morgan le Fay*'s plot to entrap Arthur with the help of her lover *Accalon of Gaul*.

Annwn (W) The British Underworld, ruled over by *Arawn*. Unlike the Classical or Christian Underworld or hell, Annwn is not considered to be a place of punishment or eternal lamentation; it is rather a place of ancestral power which mortals may visit, and from which the *Wild Hunt* rides out.

Anu (I) The mother of the gods in Ireland. The twin hills near Killarny in Munster are named the Paps of Anu after her. She is identical with *Danu*, in being the ancestress of the *Tuatha de Danaan*. [99]

Aobh (I) The first wife of *Lir*. Mother of *Fionnuala, Aed, Conn* and *Fiachna*.

Aoibhell (I) A woman of the *Sidhe* at Craig Liath in Munster. She was the tutelary spirit of the O'Briens, though in later years she was considered to be more like a *banshee* since whoever hears the music of her magical harp does not long survive the experience. She was the mistress of *Dubhlainn*.

Aoife (I) The woman-warrior who was *Scathach*'s rival. *CuChulainn* defeated her in combat and begot her with child. When she heard that he had married *Emer*, she planned her revenge. She raised his son, *Conlaoch*, in every skill and laid three *geasa* or prohibitions upon him: that he should never give way to anyone, that he should never refuse a challenge, and that he should never tell anyone his name. [5]

Aoife (I) The foster-daughter of Bodh Dearg. She married *Lir* becoming the step-mother of her sister's children, *Fionnuala, Aed, Conn* and *Fiachra*. She turned them into *swans*, destined to roam the world for 900 years. She was turned into a witch of the air, destined to sweep the winds till doomsday by Bodh Dearg. [13]

Aonbarr (I) The magical *horse* belonging to *Manannan mac Lir*. It could travel on either land or sea and was later ridden by the god *Lugh* during his quest for the Sword of Light.

Apollo (G) Originally a Thracian god, Apollo was associated with the northern land of *Hyperborea*, where he was said to winter every year. Diodorus Siculus and others supposed that this northern region was analogous with Britain.

Apollo was originally god of music, archery and hunting, as well as being a herdsman. These are also the attributes of *Mabon* or *Maponus*. Apollo's temple was identified by Diodorus as Stonehenge. Apollo was also taken up by the Romans during their occupation of Britain. Archaeological evidence suggests that Apollo's cult was already well-established under the native form of Maponus. There is a dedication to Apollo Cunomaglus or Hound-Lord, stressing his early associations rather than the later classical attributes. Apollo was also patron of *Troy* — the mythical origin of the British. [57]

Arawn (W) God of the Underworld, *Annwn*. He appears in 'Pwyll, Prince of Dyfed' as a huntsman, pursuing a white stag with a pack of red-eared hounds. He is frequently challenged by other would-be claimants for his title, 'Pen Annwn' or Head of Annwn, two such stories involve *Hafgan* and *Amatheon*. He gave *pigs* — originally underworld animals — to *Pwyll* in return for having rid him of Hafgan. He seems to cede place, seasonally, to another in order to retain his position and so is closely related to the other South Welsh God of the Underworld, *Gwynn ap Nudd*, who engages in a similar seasonal contest. [17, 80]

Ard-Greimne (I) The father of the two woman warriors who taught *Cuchulainn*, *Scathach* and *Aoife*. His name means 'High Power'.

Ardan (I) Brother of *Naoisi*, who was the lover of *Deirdriu*.

Argante (A) Queen of the Otherworld who is said to have cured *Arthur*'s wounds in Layamon's 'Brut'. The name is possibly a corruption of *Morgan le Fay* (i.e. Morgante). [31]

Arianrhod (W) Mistress of the otherworld tower of initiation, Caer Sidi, where poets learn starry wisdom and where the dead go between incarnations. She appears in the story of 'Math, Son of Mathonwy' as the daughter of *Don* and sister of *Gwydion*. When *Math* loses his footholder, she applies for the post. This involves a magical test of virginity by which she steps over Math's wand. On doing so, she gives birth to two infants; *Dylan*, and the premature *Llew*, whom Gwydion scoops up, incubates and raises as his protégé.

Having been so shamed before the whole court, Arianrhod lays a *geise* upon Llew: that he shall have no name, no arms and no human wife. All three prohibitions are overcome with the help of Gwydion's magic. The sub-text of the story and earlier references

suggest that both her children were incestuously conceived with
Gwydion her brother, or by Math, her uncle. The Corona Borealis
is named Caer Arianrhod in Welsh — the self-same constellation
which is associated with Ariadne, a Greek resonance of Arianrhod.
[17, 80]

Aries (A) A cowherd who was the supposed father of *Tor*. He
brought his son to *Arthur*'s court when the boy asked to be made
a knight. *Merlin* then revealed that Tor was in fact the son of King
Pellinore. He went on to become an excellent knight of the *Round
Table*. Aries is probably the only character in the entire Arthurian
saga who was of humble origin. [20]

Arondight (A) The sword of *Lancelot*.

Art (I) The son of *Conn Cetchathach*. He was banished from Ireland
at the request of his step-mother. *Becuma*, but returned to reign in
his father's absence. Becuma desired him secretly, but challenged
him to a game of fidchell (a game similar to chess) in which the stake
was to be the wand of *Cu Roi*. Art won and forced Becuma to obtain
this. He won the second game and had to go on a perilous quest for
Delbchaem, daughter of *Coinchend*. He overcame giants, hags and
the warrior-woman, Coinchend herself, to win Delbchaem. [6, 80]

Arthur (A) Son of *Igerna* and *Uther Pendragon*. He was brought
up by *Ector of the Forest Sauvage*, at the behest of *Merlin*. He
became King of Britain after pulling the sword from the stone. He
founded the *Round Table*, married *Guinevere* and set about making
the kingdom stable and law-abiding. During the following years his
knights rode everywhere across the land, righting wrongs and helping those in need.

The appearance of the *Grail* at *Camelot* led to a great quest in
which all the *Round Table Knights* participated. Only three were
successful however, and after this his reign began to decline. The
coming of his illegitimate son, *Mordred*, contributed to the demise
of the Round Table, as did the continuing affair between Guinevere
and the foremost of his knights, *Lancelot*. Finally Arthur met
Mordred at *Camlan*, and in the ensuing battle received a wound
which threatened his life. Three mysterious queens appeared on a
black barge and took him away to *Avalon*, to be healed, and to await
the day when he would come again.

This finalization of Arthur's myth subsumes most of the earlier
material which is extant. It is possible to find traces of a Romano-
British battle leader, a Dark Age chieftain, and a medieval king. He
succeeded to the function of *Bran* as the guardian of the realm of
Britain who could be invoked in time of need. He was said to have
been buried in *Glastonbury* Abbey where he was exhumed in the
reign of Henry II. However, tradition and popular belief credit him

with undying fame. He is said to lie sleeping in various underground caves situated at Alderly Edge in Cheshire, Richmond Castle in York-shire (see *Potter Thompson*), and Sewingshields near Hadrian's Wall, among other places. In earlier stories he appears in his own right as the central character in an adventure, in later versions his knights gradually become substitutes for their king on whose behalf they act. The stories about Arthur are called collectively 'The Matter of Britain' and remain central to the mythology of this country. [20, 28, 45, 73, 76, 77, 80, 84, 87, 100, 186]

Arthur's Bosom (A) The name sometimes given to the Otherworld in which heroes were summoned to rest after their labours. It recalled Arthur's sojourn in *Avalon*.

Arthur's Wain (A) The constellation of the Plough.

Asgard (N) Home of the Norse Gods. It was a complete world com-prising twelve regions, each ruled over by one of the gods. The most famous region was *Valhalla*, the great golden mead-hall of *Odin* where heroes came to drink and make merry. Asgard was separated from earth by a great gulf, spanned only by the rainbow bridge, *Bi-frost*. [53]

Assipattle (S) He was an idle, lie-by-the-fire lad, which is how he received his name of 'Ash-pate'. He frequently boasted of the heroic exploits he could perform, though there was little sign of these and no one believed in his talk. However, when the muckle Mester *Stoor-worm* came to ravage the country it was Assipattle who defeated it with his wit and cunning. He went to sea in a small boat, with only his knife and a bucket of burning peats. As the great sea-monster swallowed him, he cut a hole in its liver and put the burning peats inside so that he was vomited out. The Stoorworm subsequently perished, and Assipattle was wed to the king's daughter. This primal folk-hero was responsible for the creation of many northern islands because of his deed (See *Stoorworm*.) [44]

Atlantis (L) Legendary continent of great magical power, said to have existed in the Atlantic Ocean, and to have been inundated by water because of the corrupt practices of its priesthood.

  The mythology of Britain is shot through with traces of this legend. Inundations and incursions by the sea occur frequently along the western seaboard of the British Isles, while the Breton legend of the legendary city of Ys is a reflection of this legend. Atlantis represents a primal or otherworld tradition which fell through misuse of power. Legend and esoteric tradition state that survivors of Atlantis colonized parts of Britain, becoming the nucleus of its priesthood. [107]

Audhumla (N) The monstrous *cow* who spawned the first of the

Frost Giants, Ymir and the creature Burim whose son, Bor, was the father of *Odin*. She was said to have been formed from the mingling of ice from *Niflheim* and heat from *Muspellsheim*.

Avallach/Afallach (A) The father of *Modron*. King of the otherworldly kingdom of *Avalon*. [28, 80]

Avalon (A) The otherworld kingdom or Apple Island to which *Arthur* was borne to be healed of his wounds by *Morgan*.

Avenable (A) Features in a legend of *Merlin* as a girl who disguised herself as a squire and became the seneschal of the Emperor of Rome calling herself *Grisandole*. One day the Emperor had a dream in which he saw a sow with a crown on its head. He was told that only a wild man living in the woods nearby could explain the meaning of the dream.

Grisandole found the wild man, who also took the shape of a stag, and this was *Merlin*. He explained that the sow with the crown was the Empress, and that her twelve squires were in fact youths. She was summarily burned at the stake and Grisandole, revealed as a young woman, then married the Emperor! [87]

B

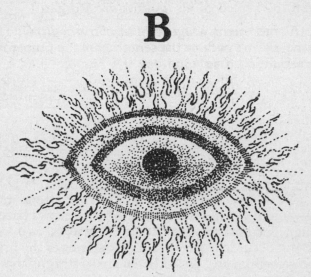

Balor's Eye

Badb (I) Crow — an aspect of the *Morrighan*. She confronted *Cuchulainn* on his way to the last battle as a *Washer at the Ford*. She likewise appeared as a harbinger of death to King *Cormac*. [5, 27, 99]

Badger (B) Famed for its tenacity and courage, the badger has entered folklore as the most unyielding animal; significantly, badger-head sporrans keep a Highlander's loose change safe. The story of *Gwawl* and *Rhiannon* shows how an ancient game 'Badger in the Bag' was supposed to have originated, but traces of this custom, called 'Beat the Badger' in Fife, show how it may have been a form of ancient ordeal, a running the gauntlet, where the player ran between a double line of boys wielding sticks. [80, 183]

Balan (A) Brother of *Balin*. The two slew each other unknowingly while wearing borrowed armour as a disguise.

Balder/Baldur (N) Called 'the Beautiful'. Balder was the God of Light, son of *Odin* and *Frigga*, twin brother of *Hodur*. The best-loved of the gods, he was slain by the blind Hodur who was tricked into throwing a spear of mistletoe at his brother, by *Loki*. It was known that Balder was impervious to all wounds save that inflicted by this wood. Odin sent *Hermod* into the Underworld to bring Balder back but he was unsuccessful. [53]

Balin (A) Brother of *Balan*. He is sometimes called 'le Sauvage'. He slew *Arthur*'s cousin and was imprisoned. On being released, he rode out on an adventure, in which he killed the evil knight, *Garlon*, while staying at the castle of his brother, King *Pelles*. Pursued through the castle by the angry monarch, Balin accidentally wounded the king through both thighs with the spear of the *Hallows*. This action was called the '*Dolorous Blow*', and is said to have caused the *Wasteland*. (See *Wounded King*.) [20]

Balor (I) King of the *Fomorians*. It was prophesied that his grandson would kill him and so he kept his daughter secluded on an island. But *Cian mac Cainte* was able to visit the island where he slept with *Ethniu*, Balor's daughter. Of their union *Lugh* was born.

Balor was one-eyed because he had spied on some druids who were preparing a draught of wisdom. Some splashed out and hit him in the eye thus making the glance of this eye baleful to any he looked upon. He kept that eye-lid closed and had four attendants to raise it when he wanted to kill his enemies. At the second Battle of Mag Tuired, Lugh put out this eye with a sling-stone and killed him. Traces of Balor occur in many extant folk-stories of the British Isles. Parallels between him and *Yspaddaden* are so striking that it is clear they are analogous with each other. [5, 149]

Banba (I) According to a lost early manuscript, she was the first settler in Ireland which was called 'the island of Banba of the women' — which perhaps is associated with *Tir na mBan*. She was one of the three goddesses of *Sovereignty* to whom *Amergin* promised the honour of naming the island after her. [15]

Banshee/Bean Sidhe (I) The Woman of the *Sidhe*. Traditionally she is associated with the coming death of a person in families which retain some links with the Otherworld, and who have a resident banshee who warns of a death. She is associated with the *Washer at the Ford*.

Barinthus (A) Called the 'Navigator', he guided *Merlin* and *Taliesin* on their voyage to the otherworld island with the wounded *Arthur*. He epitomizes the ferryman of the dead and may be drawn from the mythos of *Manannan*. He is also, in the form of St Barrind, responsible for starting Saint *Brendan* on his voyage to the paradise of the Blest. (See *Fortunate Islands*.) [19, 22, 76]

Baruch (I) The Red Branch warror who met *Deirdre* and *Naoisi* on their return from Scotland. He persuaded *Fergus* to leave his guarding of the runaway couple in order to feast with himself. Fergus, one of whose geise included the inability not to respond to any hospitality offered to him, complied, thus leaving the doomed couple to their fate.

Baudwin of Brittany (A) One of the best of the later Knights of the *Round Table*, he survived the last battle of *Camlan* and lived thereafter as a hermit. He was also known for his skill as a surgeon.

Bear (B) Although no longer native to these islands, the bear has remained one of Britain's totem beasts at a deep level. An old Gaelic proverb, 'Art an neart', describes a hero as a bear in vigour. *Arthur's* own name derives from the British 'arth' or bear. The constellation of the Plough or the Great Bear is also called *Arthur's Wain*.

Beare (I) A princess of Spain who married *Eoghan Mor*. It was prophesied that her destined husband would appear to her if she went one night to the River Eibhear where she found a *salmon* arrayed in brilliant robes. The Beare peninsula on the south-west tip of Ireland is named in her honour. (See *Cailleach Bheare*.)

Beast Glatisant (A) See *Questing Beast*.

Beaumains (A) See *Gareth of Orkney*.

Becuma (I) An otherworldly woman, exiled from *Tir Tairngire* for an unspecified transgression. She lusted after *Art*, but married his father, *Conn Cetchathach* because he was king. The union was ill-fated because she did not rightfully represent *Sovereignty*, and the land was without milk or corn.

She made Conn banish Art, but when he returned to reign in his father's stead she challenged him to a game of fidchell (chess). Art won the first game and demanded she obtain the wand of *Cu Roi*. She won the second game and made Art seek for *Delbchaem*. When Art successfully returned with his new bride, he banished Becuma from Tara. [6, 99]

Bedwyr/Bedivere (A) One of the earliest figures associated with *Arthur*. He may once have had a role similar to that of *Lancelot* who replaced him in the later romances where he is chiefly remembered for being the knight to whom Arthur entrusted the relinquishing of *Excalibur*. He was Arthur's butler. [28, 84, 20]

Befind (I) *Midir's* name for *Etain* when she was his wife in the *Sidhe*.

Beheading Game (A) The game in which a mysterious challenger — usually a giant, or *Green Knight* — enters the hall during wintertime and offers his axe to any hero who will cut off his head in return for a similar beheading blow. A hero accepts and finds that the challenger rises and immediately picks up the axe and demands the right to return the blow.

In the case of *Gawain*, he was allowed a year's grace to receive the return blow. In the case of *CuChulainn*, he knelt immediately and was judged the bravest knight of Ulster. The game is clearly part of the mid-winter festivities in which the old year enters as the giant or Green Knight, the old spirit of the forest, and is challenged by the one representing the new year in its strength and hardiness. [5, 14, 25]

Bel (C) See *Bile*.

Belatucadros (C) Celtic war-god reverenced in Northern Britain, whom the Romans associated with *Mars*. His name means 'Fair Shining One', and he is the horned god of the north. [59, 103, 119]

Belinus (L) Brother of Brennius. King of Britain. He quarrelled with his brother but they were eventually reconciled and together they sacked Rome. He built many roads and established his capital at Caer Usk. He built Billingsgate in Trinovantum (London) and was buried there in a golden urn. [9]

Bellieus (A) Unfortunate knight in the early adventures of *Lancelot*. *Lancelot* accidentally entered the tent in which Bellieus' lady was sleeping and got into bed beside her. Bellieus, returning suddenly, found Lancelot and challenged him, with the inevitable result that he was almost fatally wounded. However, he survived, and was later made a knight of the *Round Table*.

Beltaine (C) The Celtic feast of May-Eve, celebrated on the evening of April 30. It marked the beginning of Summer, when livestock was let out of winter pasture to crop the new greenness of Spring. The word means literally 'the fire of Bel', a deity related to *Belinus*. At this feast, all household fires were doused and rekindled from the new fire which the druids built on this night. (See *Lughnasadh*, *Oimelc* and *Samhain*.)

Bendith y Mamau (W) 'The Mothers' Blessing'. The euphemistic name for the *Fairies* in Wales. It is significant that they are associated with the triple form of the Goddess. (See *Mothers*.)

Beowulf (N) Perhaps the most famous of all heroes, his story is told in an eighth-century poem written in the West Saxon dialect of Old English. It combines three major stories, which tell of Beowulf's battle with the monster, *Grendel*, whom he maimed after a wrestling match. The second story tells of his struggle with Grendel's mother — a water-troll — beneath the waters of a lake; and the third tells of his combat with a *dragon* in which Beowulf received a fatal wound. These stories were probably part of a longer cycle of hero-tales current in Saxon countries. [53, 162]

Bercelak/Bertilak (A) See *Green Knight*.

Bevis of Hampton (L) Son of Sir Guy of Hampton (Southampton). He was sent to the East and was enslaved, but married a sultan's daughter, killed a *dragon* and befriended a giant called Ascapard. Bevis is also associated with Arundel Castle in Sussex, where his sword, Morglay, is still kept. [98]

Bifrost (N) The rainbow bridge of the gods, stretching between earth and *Asgard*, made of fire, air and water. It is destined to break at *Ragnarok* when the invading giants walk upon it. *Thor*, the largest of the gods, was forbidden to tread upon it. [53]

Bile (I) The Celtic world understood an archetype roughly equivalent to the powerful lord of life and death. In British tradition he was called *Bel* or *Belinus*, but in Irish he was Bile. In some texts, he is said to come to Ireland from Spain — which is clearly intended to be the Land of the Dead. The fires of *Beltaine* were lit to mark his recognized feast. Very little is known of his mythos, but he, like *Danu* who is sometimes named as his consort, was a powerful ancestral deity to the Celtic races.

Black Annis (L) A blue-faced hag, akin to the *Cailleachs Bheare* and *Bheur*, who eat people. She is supposed to live in a cave in the Dane Hills in Leicestershire. It has been suggested that she is associated with *Anu* or *Danu*. [78]

Blackbird (B) The blackbird has ever been one of Britain's most melodious songsters and this is doubtless why the Birds of *Rhiannon* are said to be three blackbirds: they sing on the branch of the everlasting otherworldly tree which grows in the centre of the earthly paradise. Their singing entranced the hearer, ushering him or her into the Otherworld. They sing for *Bran* and the Company of the Noble Head, in their feasting between the worlds. The blackbird is also responsible for the finding of *Mabon*. [80]

Bladud (I) King of Britain who built Caer Badum (Bath). He established the temple to *Minerva* at Bath and, having discovered the medicinal qualities of the waters, caused the baths to be attached to the temple-precincts. He made wings and crashed to his death from the Temple of *Apollo* in Trinovantum. His mythos is similar to that of *Abaris*, and he seems to embody the traditions of both priest and king in one. [9, 114]

Blaise (A) The shadowy figure who stands behind *Merlin*. Described as his teacher, Blaise retired to Northumberland where Merlin often visited him and where his deeds and prophecies were recorded. [26]

Blanaid/Blathnat (I) The wife of *Cu Roi mac Daire* who came originally from the Otherworld, and who fell to him as the spoils of war. She secretly loved *CuChulainn* and enabled him to murder Cu Roi by entangling his hair, Delilah-like, to the bedstead. She was killed by Cu Roi's poet who avenged his lord by throwing himself off a high place clasping the faithless Blanaid. Her name means 'flower' and she is analogous to *Blodeuwedd*. [5, 76, 80]

Blanchfleur (A) The name sometimes given to *Perceval*'s sister. She gave her life to heal a leprous woman and her body accompanied the *Grail Questers* to *Sarras*. (See *Dindraine*.)

Blessed Islands (C) The group of otherworldly islands which lie west of Ireland, wherein the worthy dead and otherworldly folk live in the Celtic earthly paradise.

Blodeuwedd (W) The Flower-Bride of *Llew*, formed out of flowers, blossom, and nine separate elements by *Gwydion* and *Math*, in order to circumvent the geise laid upon Llew by *Arianrhod*. She was never asked whether she loved Llew and soon fell in love with a passing hunter, *Gronw Pebr*, with whom she plotted her husband's death.
   Like Delilah, she coaxed the destined cause of death from Llew and then entrapped him by enacting the conditions exactly. She was then punished by Gwydion, by being turned into an *owl* — the night-hunting bird which is mobbed and shunned by all day-time fowls. Her story follows a well-known folk motif: that of the betraying Flower-Bride, a role she shares with both *Blanaid* and *Guinevere*. [17, 80]

Boann/Board (I) Goddess of the river Boyne, wife of *Elcmar*, mother of *Angus*. Her name means 'She of the White Cows'. The *Dagda* desired her and sent Elcmar on an errand which lasted nine months, although it was made to seem like one day. [19, 42]

Boar (B) The wild boar, once commonly hunted throughout the British Isles is now only to be found in remote areas of Europe. The ferocity and cunning of the animal made him a dangerous quarry, yet the art and literature of Celtic peoples attest to his importance in their mythology. *Twrch Trwyth* appears in the 'Mabinogion' as a devastating foe to *Arthur* and his kingdom; this boar is paralleled in Irish tradition by *Orc Triath*. A white boar leads *Pryderi* into slavery in *Annwn*, while a similar animal is the cause of *Diarmuid's* death. [80]

Bodach (S) Literally, 'old man'. It was a Highland belief that the Bodach would creep down chimneys and steal naughty children, although in other parts it was considered to be a death-warning spirit. It is interesting to note that, unlike his likely counterpart, the *Cailleach*, the Bodach has no body of folklore or mythos to support it. [44]

Bodb (I) King of the Sidi of Munster. Son of the *Dagda*. He assisted

Angus in the finding of *Caer Ibormeith*. It was to his kingdom that *Lir* retired. [13, 19]

Bors de Ganis (A) Son of King Ban of Benoic. *Lancelot*'s cousin and one of the best known of the Knights of the *Round Table*. Together with *Perceval* and *Galahad*, he was one of the three successful *Grail Questers*. [24, 83]

Boudicca/Boadicea (C) (d. AD 62) Queen of the Iceni. When her husband, Prasutagus, died leaving half his kingdom to the Romans, she discovered that the Romans intended to take the whole kingdom for themselves. After scourging Boudicca and raping her two daughters, the Romans were to suffer the worst native rebellion since they conquered Britain. Sacking Colchester and London, Boudicca and her tribesmen ravaged the countryside until finally she was overcome by Suetonius Paulinus, when, to avoid being paraded in a Roman triumph as a captive queen, she is said to have taken poison. She was a devotee of *Andraste*, the goddess of victory, to whom she sacrificed her captives. She is fondly remembered, despite the bloodiness of rebellion, as an example of liberation to captive peoples — a concept dear to the hearts of all Britons. [187]

Brahan Seer (d.1577) Coinneach Odhar was a man who had the gift of sight into the future. His prophecies concerning the Battle of Culloden, the Highland Clearances and the coming of the railways were all borne out, as was his series of prophecies concerning the Seaforth family. He informed the Countess of Seaforth that her husband was unfaithful to her and she had him hideously burned to death in a tar-barrel, but not before he foretold the dying out of the Seaforth line, which would end with a man both deaf and dumb. This was indeed fulfilled. [98, 120]

Bran mac Febal (I) An otherworld woman invited Bran to set sail for the *Blessed Islands* where he would find the Land of Women (*Tir na mBan*). While on the sea, he encountered *Manannan mac Lir* who told him of the delights of *Mag Mell* and *Tir Tairngire*. When Bran came to the Land of Women he was entertained royally and invited to remain, becoming an immortal, but one of his crew became homesick and they sailed back to Ireland, only to find that Bran had become the stuff of legend, as many years had passed in the Otherworld. [19]

Bran the Blessed/Bendigeid Fran (W) The Titanic-sized Bran has become deeply incorporated into British mythology. His story appears in 'Branwen Daughter of Llyr' where he is the possessor of a life-restoring *cauldron*. On the marriage of his sister, *Branwen* to *Matholwch*, King of Ireland, he gives up the cauldron to the Irish, in recompense for the insults they have suffered at the hands of

Bran's brother, *Efnissien*. He subsequently has to rescue Branwen from her servitude in the Irish King's kitchen after he has her imprisoned there. He wades across the Irish sea, leading the British fleet and defeats the Irish who offer to depose Matholwch and make *Gwern*, Branwen's son, king in his place.

At the feast to celebrate the truce and Gwern's accession, Efnissien throws Gwern into the fire and hostilities are resumed. The Irish resuscitate their dead in the cauldron, but neither side is triumphant; only seven Britons escape alive but Bran is mortally wounded in the heel. He requests that his head be cut off and buried at the White Tower (of London). The seven survivors do so, first bearing the head to Harlech for seven years and then to Gwales (Grassholm, Pembrokeshire) for eighty years, where the head of Bran converses with them and where they have no sense of time passing, nor of the happenings they have experienced. They are asked not to open the door of the hall. Eventually one of the company does so and they become aware of the passing of time and of their sufferings.

Bran's mythos can be traced to that of *Cronos*, as well as becoming incorporated into the *Grail* legends where *Brons* is the guardian of the Grail — a development of the life-restoring cauldron. The Triads relate how *Arthur* dug up Bran's head where it had been set to fend off enemy invasion, because he alone wished to be his country's bastion. This feature can still be seen in the legend that if the *ravens* leave the Tower of London Britain will be invaded (for which reason their wings are kept clipped). Bran's name means 'raven'. [17, 28, 80]

Brandubh (I) He was King of Leinster in the seventh century who lusted after *Mongan*'s wife, Dubh Lacha. He tricked Mongan into giving her up, but was finally defeated by Mongan's supernatural powers. The name is also that of an Irish boardgame, meaning Black Raven, played between two players.

Brangaine (A) *Iseult*'s maid who helped her dupe King *Mark* by sleeping with him on her mistress' wedding knight. She also administered the love-potion to *Tristan* and Iseult (according to some versions) which was intended for Mark and Iseult. It bound the lovers together forever. [20]

Branwen (W) Daughter of *Llyr*, sister of *Bran*. She was married to *Matholwch*, King of Ireland, and bore him *Gwern*, but the Irish people bade Matholwch put her away because of the insults they had suffered at the hands of *Efnissien*, her brother. She was made to serve in the kitchens and was there struck by the cook. She tamed a starling to bear a message to Bran in Britain who came with a fleet to rescue her. Efnissien threw Gwern upon the fire and after the ensuing battle between the British and Irish, she died of a broken heart and was buried in a 'four-sided grave' on the river Alaw, in Anglesey. Her mythos bears a striking resemblance to that of *Cordelia*, also a daughter of *Lear*. Branwen is a type of *Sovereignty*, as becomes obvious if this story is investigated thoroughly. [17, 80]

Brastias (A) Originally a knight in the service of *Gorlois* of *Cornwall*, Brastias became an ally of *Merlin* in the episode where *Uther* is changed into the likeness of his master in order to sleep with *Igraine*. When *Arthur* became King, Brastias was one of his first and most able captains, and became Warden of the North. [20]

Breasil (I) Was considered to be the King of the World in Irish tradition and although a fortress was supposed to have been built by him in Leinster, his real dwelling was in the lands to the west, called *Hy Breasil*, the otherwordly place whose name was used in the mapping of South America as Brazil.

Bregon (I) Scythian noble, ancestor of the *Milesians*. He was exiled from Egypt and settled in Spain from whence his two sons, *Ith* and *Bile* set sail for Ireland. [15]

Saint Brendan (I) (c.489–583) Born in Kerry, this saint takes his place in Irish legend for his wondrous voyages to the Promised Land of Saints — a christianized version of the Blessed Isles of the West. He was inspired to take this voyage by Saint Barrind (see *Barinthus*) who had just returned from there. Together with seventeen monks, Brendan set sail in a skin-covered boat and spent many years travelling from island to island, including a hazardous landing on a whale, where he said mass and his monks attempted to heat a *cauldron*. There are many parallels and overlaps with the voyage of *Maelduine*. [22]

Brennius (L) Brother of *Belinus*, with whom he quarrelled and fought. Both were reconciled by their mother, Tonuuenna, and together they marched on Gaul which they conquered, and then besieged Rome which Brennius sacked. [9]

Bres mac Elatha (I) The son of *Eriu*, begotten of her by an otherworld youth, *Elatha* who was of the *Fomorians*. Eriu herself was of the *Tuatha de Danaan*. Although he was a child of mixed parentage, he was elected king on the understanding that he would relinquish sovereignty if any misdeed should give cause. But Bres treated his mother's people poorly, inflicting grave insults upon the Tuatha.

He created a monopoly over the food supplies of Ireland, making the Tuatha obliged to serve him in order to be fed. He was then satirized by the Tuatha's poet. (A poet's satire could cause personal disfigurement, in the case of Bres the King, he was considered maimed and therefore unfit to reign.)

Eventually the Tuatha rose against him and Bres joined the

Fomorian side during the second Battle of Mag Tuired. Here he bargained with *Lugh* in a magical contest which he lost. He was forced to drink 300 buckets of tainted milk and died. [5]

Breuse sans Pitie (A) The knight who became a byword in the Arthurian world as the most thoroughly evil-hearted villain living at that time. He captured and killed many of *Arthur*'s knights, and was responsible for the discomfiture of many others. He does not seem to have ever been either caught or punished for his crimes — unusual in the Arthurian world — but simply fades from the scene in the various texts which mention him. [20]

Brian (I) With his brothers *Iuchar* and *Iucharba*, the sons of *Tuirenn*, he slew *Cian mac Cainte*, the father of *Lugh*. Lugh discovered the body of Cian, exhumed it and then set out to avenge him. He ordered that the sons of Tuirenn should pay an impossible compensation for their crime, including the three apples of the *Hesperides* and many other otherwordly treasures. They obtained everything asked by Lugh but died at last in the achieving of the last task.

There is an obvious overlay between this story and that of *Culhwch*, who performed impossible tasks for *Yspaddaden*. Lugh's lack of mercy in not sparing the sons of Tuirenn is like that of *Llew* to his wife's lover, *Gronw Pebr*. [5, 13]

Brian Boru (926–1014) King of Ireland. He successfully defeated the almost universal scourge of the Danes which afflicted Ireland and Britain at that time, at the Battle of Clontarf, however, he lost his own life in the process.

Like *Alfred the Great*, he liked to do his own reconnoitring. On one such foray, he encountered an Irish woman crying because her Danish husband had bidden her kill her child for food, there being none to cook due to the ravages of war. Brian gave her food and in return she was able to give the password of the stronghold, which enabled him to overcome his foe. He was said to have introduced the plover into Ireland because of its facility for warning of enemy attack. [90]

Briareus (G) According to Plutarch, Briareus was the hundred-handed giant set to guard *Cronos* in *Ogygia*, a mystical island in the Atlantic Ocean. [57]

Bricriu (I) Satirist and mischief-maker at *Conchobar*'s court. He incited rivalry between the heroes *CuChulainn*, *Conall* and *Loegaire* by assigning the 'hero's portion' of the feast to the best warrior. The champions' three wives were driven to contend for the place of honour. The dispute was settled by *Cu Roi mac Daire* who offered the heroes a chance of playing the *beheading game*; only CuChulainn would play it and so won the contest. Bricriu was surnamed Nemthenga or Poison-Tongue. [5, 12]

Brigantia (C) Titular goddess of the Brigantes, of the West Riding in Yorkshire. A dedication and bas-relief at Birrens depicts her with the victorious attributes of *Minerva* and wearing the mural crown of Cybele, which shows how the Romans adopted her into their own mythos. Natively, she was a goddess of water and of pastoral activities. She may be equated with the Irish Brigit. [97]

Brigit/Brigid/Bride (I) Daughter of the *Dagda*. In her triple aspect she was patroness of poets, healers and smiths. Her son by *Bres*, *Ruadan*, was slain by *Goibnui*. For him she made the first keening that was ever heard in Ireland.

She was subsumed in the cult and person of Saint Brigit of Kildare (450–523) who founded the first female religious community after Christianity had been established in Ireland. The sanctuary of the nunnery at Kildare had a perpetual fire, tended by the sisterhood, which was not extinguished until the Reformation. Saint Brigit is the secondary patron saint of Ireland.

Within Scottish tradition Brigid (the saint and the goddess) is associated with the lambing season and the coming of spring, when she ousts the winter reign of the *Cailleach Bheur*. The saint is further known as the 'Mary of the Gael' and is credited with being the midwife to the Virgin. A folk-story tells how she played the fool by lighting a crown of candles and wearing it on her head to distract Herod's soldiers from the Holy Infant. Traces of Brigit can be discerned in *Brigantia*. [5, 48, 78]

Brisen (A) Described in Malory's 'Le Morte d'Arthur' as 'one of the greatest enchantresses that was at that time in the world living.' She engineered the coming together of *Lancelot* and *Elaine of Corbenic* to engender *Galahad*, by giving Lancelot drugged wine and then leading him to Elaine's room having first convinced him that it contained *Guinevere*. [20]

Britannia (RB) Whenever the Romans occupied a new colony they were careful to propitiate the genius of the land. Britannia was the personified genia of Britain and was first depicted on a coin of Antoninus Pius (d. AD161). Latterly, Britannia, with the attributes and weapons of *Minerva*, appeared on coins during the reign of Charles II in 1665, and became the symbol of the British Empire. She is the last remaining personification of Britain's native *Sovereignty*.

Broceliande (A) The great Arthurian world-forest in which most of the adventures of the *Round Table* took place. It is actually situated in Brittany where many related Arthurian sites can be visited. [37]

Brollachan (S) One of the most feared spirits of the Highland, because it was shapeless. Tradition has it that it could only speak two phrases: 'Myself' and 'Thyself'. It took the shape of whatever it sat upon, but apart from that had only a mouth and eyes. [44]

Brons (A) Also called Hebron, he was the son-in-law of *Joseph of Arimathea* and the grandfather of *Perceval*. One of the first *Grail Kings*, to be called *Fisher King*, he has been plausibly identified with the Welsh god *Bran the Blessed*. [82, 83]

Brownies (S) Domestic spirits in the form of small men wearing brown attire. They do the housework in return for a bowl of milk, but they must never be offered any reward else they are driven away.

Bruno le Noir (A) Also dubbed 'La Cote Male-Taile' by Sir *Kay* because of his ill-fitting clothes. He came to *Camelot* as a poor man and was made a scullion. After many adventures he married the damsel *Maledisant* and became the Overlord of Pendragon Castle. He shares many of the attributes of *Gareth* and is probably a later shadow of the Orkney knight.

Brutus (L) The great-grandson of Aeneas. He accidentally killed his father and fled from Italy to Greece, where he became the acknowledged leader of the enslaved Trojans. He led them away and, having been instructed by Diana while sleeping her temple, sailed to Britain where he founded a second *Troy* — Troia Nova (Trinovantum) on the banks of the Thames. He defeated an army of giants and chained their leaders, Gog and Magog, to be his porters (see *Gogmagog*). Alternatively, according to Geoffrey of Monmouth, *Corineus* threw the giant Gogmagog into the sea. He is remembered as the ancestor of the Britons. [9]

Budoc (ST) His mother, Azenor, was thrown into the English Channel while pregnant, by her step-mother who believed her to be unfaithful to her husband. The unfortunate woman was sustained by visions of *Saint Brigit* and was brought ashore in Waterford, Ireland, where she became a washerwoman at the monastery. Here Budoc grew up, later becoming the Bishop of Dol in Brittany. He is the patron of Budock in Cornwall. His feast-day is 8 December.

Buggane (C) Manx goblin which can change its shape, and which is vicious, delighting in undoing the work of human beings.

Bull (B) A primal symbol of strength and potency, the bull is a frequent figure in British mythology. It is possible that the bull was a special totemic animal of kingly rule and that sacred herds of cattle played a prominent part in ancient rituals. The 'Tarbh-feis,' or bull-feast was perhaps a remnant of this understanding: among the Gaelic peoples, a white bull was slaughtered and a druid would drink of its blood and eat its flesh in preparation for sleeping wrapped in the flayed hide. His subsequent dreams would determine the rightful king to be elected. The bull is the central cause of the 'Tain Bo Cuailgne' (Cattle Raid of Cooley). The Isle of Man is haunted by the Tarroo-Ushtey or Water Bull, which, similar to the *each-uisge* is a beast to be avoided or treated with caution for it can drag mortals into the sea and drown them. The bull is also the shape into which a knight is enchanted in the folk-story, 'the Black Bull of Norroway.' [172, 185, 186]

Bwca (W) Like the Scottish *Brownies*, a domestic spirit which does the housework in return for food.

C

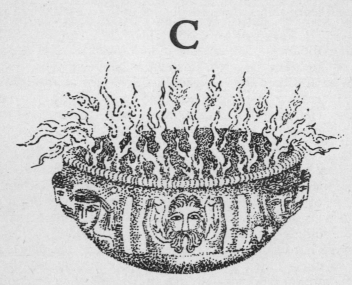

Cauldron

Cabal/Caval (A) King *Arthur*'s hound. It is said to have left the print of a paw on a certain stone in Wales, which though moved from its resting place at night, always returns by the morning.

Cabyll-Ushtey (C) The Manx version of the *each-uisge*. It was just as treacherous, pulling men and animals to their deaths. (See *Kelpie*.)

Caedmon (ST) (d.680) He was a herdsman at Whitby, unlettered and simple. He suddenly discovered that he could compose poetry and songs, and wrote a series of these about the Creation, the early history of the Israelites and the last things. He came to the attention of Saint *Hilda* of Whitby, who encouraged him. He became a monk and was venerated on 11 February. Only nine lines of his poetry survive in Bede.

Caer Ibormeith (I) Daughter of Ethal Anubal, beloved of *Angus*. She was called 'a powerful, many-shaped girl', because of her ability to change her shape. She spent one year in human form and alternate years in the form of a *swan*. [19, 99]

Cai (A) See *Kay*.

Cailleach Bheur (S) The blue-faced hag who represents the season of winter. She was reborn every *Samhain* (31 October) and caused snow to fall. Her power was broken by the appearance of *Brigit*, as the spirit of springtime during February, and she laid aside her staff under a holly bush and turned into a stone at *Beltaine* (30 April). Her son was the god of youth, analogous to *Mabon* and *Angus mac Og*, whom she chased in endless combat. She is analogous to *Cailleach Bheare* and is undoubtedly one of the most ancient aspects of the Goddess in the British Isles. (See *Black Annis*.) [48, 78]

Cailleach Bheare (I) The ancient mountain mother of the south-west of Ireland. South-west Munster was believed to be the abode of the dead and here the Cailleach had lived for countless ages so that her successive husbands died of old age while she enjoyed endless youth. Her legend persists in north-west Scotland and the Isle of Man, where she is believed to control the winter months of the year and the weather. (See *Cailleach Bheur*.) [78, 99]

Caillagh ny Groamagh (C) The Old Gloomy Woman is a Manx version of the *Cailleach Beare/Bheur*. She is primarily associated with the change of the weather. Tradition tells that if Saint *Brigit*'s Day (1 February) is fine, she will emerge to gather sticks to warm herself during the summer, but if it is wet she remains indoors and has therefore to work harder at making the rest of the year fine. She is sometimes seen as giant bird carrying sticks; a remembrance of the great mountain mother who flew through the air laying down mountain ranges in primeval memory. [44]

Cairenn (I) The concubine of Eochu, mother of *Niall*. She was made to serve at the well by *Mongfind*, Eochu's first wife, and there gave birth to Niall whom she feared to nurture because of Mongfind's jealousy. However, the poet Torna fostered Niall and presented the boy to his father. Cairenn was then released from menial work and clothed in the royal purple. Niall's recognition of his mother, before all other considerations, rightly enabled him to encounter *Sovereignty* with a kiss instead of abhorrence. Cairenn is herself an earthly representative of Sovereignty. [6]

Cairpre Liffechair (I) He exterminated the *Fianna* at the Battle of Gabhra where he killed *Oscar*, *Fionn*'s grandson. He was the son of *Cormac mac Art*. He was himself killed at the Battle of Gabhra. [6, 8]

Calatin (I) *CuChulainn* killed Calatin and his sons at the ford, but Calatin's wife had three daughters, each with one eye, who avenged their family. They were skilled in enchantment and caused CuChulainn to see and hear a phantom host fighting against his countrymen which spurred him on to his death at the hands of *Lugaid*, whom they helped. [12]

Caledfwlch (A) See *Excalibur*.

Caliburnus (A) See *Excalibur*.

Camber (L) Second son of *Brutus*, after whom Wales or Cambria is named. [9]

Camelot (A) *Arthur*'s chief city and the capital of *Logres*. Said to have been built by *Merlin* in a single night, it has been ascribed to many sites, the most popular being Cadbury Camp in Somerset.

Camlan (A) The site of the terrible last battle between the forces of *Arthur* and those of *Mordred*, in which most of the *Round Table Knights* were killed. Identified by some authors with Camelford, Somerset or with Cambogianna (Birdoswald).

Camulos (C) Belgic war-god, eponymous deity of Camulodunum (Colchester). Coins bearing his name have the symbol of the *boar* upon them.

Caoilte mac Ronan (I) One of the *Fianna*, and their best runner. He released *Fionn* from imprisonment by gathering two of every wild beast for his ransom.

Caoineag (S) The Scottish version of the *banshee*. It is said that she was heard wailing the night before the massacre of Glencoe.

Caradoc Briefbras (A) Caradoc of the Withered or Short Arm. He features as the hero of the roman 'Livre de Caradoc' and as one of *Arthur*'s knights in Welsh tradition. His name stems from a mis-reading of the Old Welsh 'freichfras' meaning 'strong arm'. [87]

Carannog (ST) (sixth century) legend tells how he subdued a ser-pent being hunted by *Arthur*, this was despite the fact that the King had removed the saint's altar for use as a dinner-table. Arthur restored it to him. [16]

Caswallawn (W) Welsh king, son of *Beli Mawr*. In popular memory, Cassivellaunos, the Belgic king of the Catuvellauni, who had led the tribes against Caesar in 54 BC survived as Caswallawn. The 'Triads' cite him as being the suitor of *Fflur*, and remember him as one of the three golden shoemakers, along with *Manawyddan* and *Llew*. In 'Branwen, Daughter of Llyr', he conquers Britain in the absence of *Bran*, by means of his magic mantle. (See *Thirteen Treasures of Britain*.) [17, 28, 80]

Cat (B) The cat is now so domesticated it seems impossible to imagine mythical Britain being ravaged by a giant wild-cat, but so it was, until *Arthur* and *Cai* overcame it, according to an early Welsh text. Indeed the cat has not been necessarily appreciated for its virtues in British folklore where it often appears as the totem of black witches. One unpleasant form of divination among the Scottish Gaels was 'taghgairm', by which a live cat was spitted over a fire until other cats appeared to relieve its distress by answering the question set by the operator of this method. Among the Gaelic peoples it was a powerful totem of many tribes. Caithness is named from the clan of the Catti, or cat-people, while in Ireland, *Fionn* fought against a tribe of 'cat-heads' — possibly warriors with catskin over their helmets. [44, 183]

Cath Sith (S) The Cat of the *Sidhe*: a fairy cat. Highlanders believed that the Cait Sith was really a transformed witch not a fairy. The King of this otherworldly company of cats was called Big Ears and he would appear to answer questions set by a dinner engaged in taghairm – the roasting of a cat over fire. (See *Cat.*) [44]

Cathbad (I) The druid of *Conchobar mac Nessa* and his father. He prophesied that the boy who took arms on a certain day would outstrip all of Ireland's heroes. *CuChulainn* heard him and 'took valour' as a warrior that day, although he was but a boy. Cathbad also foretold the sorrow which *Deirdriu* would cause Conchobar and the whole of Ulster. [5, 12, 99]

Cathubodua (C) This Celtic goddess of war's name means Battle-Crow. Inscriptions have been found to her in Europe, but she is undoubtedly associated with *Badh* or Bodh, the Irish battle-goddess. [185]

Cauldron (C) In ancient Celtic myth there were several cauldrons dispensing variously the properties of life, death, inspiration and wisdom. It is generally understood that these gave way in time to the image of the Holy *Grail* and became incorporated into the *Hallows* of Britain. *Arthur* went in search of such a cauldron to the very gates of *Annwn*. *Bran* possessed a cauldron which re-animated dead men. In the story of *Taliesin*, *Ceridwen* owned a cauldron which gave inspiration. [80, 82, 83, 103]

Ceasg (S) The Scottish mermaid. Her body was that of a maiden while her tail was that of a young *salmon*. She was able to grant three wishes, if captured and could only be overcome by the destruction of her soul, which was normally kept elsewhere, in an object or land-feature. (See *Merrow*.)

Celidon/Cellydon/Cat Coit Celidon (A) The name of the great forest of Arthurian Britain, site of one of *Arthur*'s battles. *Merlin* was said to have wandered there in his madness. [29, 111]

Celtchair (I) He was a Red Branch warrior who, in the act of slaying his adulterous wife's lover, let fall a drop of blood upon the fidchell (chess) board which *Conchobar mac Nessa* and *CuChulainn* were

playing at. This was a breach of hospitality for which Celtchair was
ordered to perform three separate feats to rid Ireland of three plagues.
He had to kill *Cu Roi mac Daire*'s brother, *Conganchas*, who was
devastating the land but who was invulnerable to ordinary weapons.
He learned from Conganchas' wife, *Niamh*, that her husband could
be slain only by having spear-tips thrust into the soles of his feet.
The second plague was an otherworldly dog which he slew. The last
plague was another dog who he dispatched but whose venomous
blood trickled from Conganchas' spear on to him, by which he died.
[5]

Ceridwen (W) Goddess of inspiration. She represents the *Cailleach*
or hag-aspect of the goddess, in her guise as initiator. By her husband, *Tegid Foel*, she had two children: the most beautiful *Creirwy*,
her daughter, and *Afagddu*, her most ugly son. In order to compensate him for his appearance, she prepared a *cauldron* of knowledge and set an old man to stir it and a young boy, *Gwion Bach*,
to fetch wood.
   At the end of the year's preparations for the brew, some of the
liquid landed upon Gwion's finger, gifting him with knowledge.
Ceridwen pursued him in many guises until at last he became a grain
of wheat and she a hen. Scrabbling him up into her crop, she swallowed him, giving birth to him nine months later. She set him adrift
in a leather bag or coracle into a river, whence he was subsequently
discovered and recognized as the poet, *Taliesin*. [17, 80, 83]

Cernunnos (C) His name means 'Horned One', and he is the Lord
of the Beasts. He is frequently depicted with one or more ram-headed
serpents, and has a torc of chieftainship about his neck. Some reliefs
show him with coin-filled purses. Since both metal and snakes are
chthonic symbols, it follows that Cernunnos was associated with
the Underworld as well as with earthly fertility. (See *Wild Herdsman* and *Belatucadros*.) [103]

Cessair (I) She was the first settler in Ireland before the Flood. She
came with fifty women and three men. When her father *Fintan*, disappeared and her husband died she herself died of grief. She was
followed by all her women. Forty days after their arrival in Ireland
the Flood came. Only Fintan escaped, hiding in a cave. [15]

Charles I (1600–49) King of Britain and Ireland. The grandson of
Mary Queen of Scots, Charles was well steeped in the misfortunes
of the Stuarts. He upheld the Divine Right of Kings, by which the
mystical destiny of the king under God gave him sovereign power
in governing his country. He was deposed by Oliver Cromwell and
the Parliamentarians and executed. His was one of the latest in the
role of kingly sacrifices, whose cult was popularly acclaimed and
liturgically approved. His remembrance, on 30 January, was ordered

by his son Charles II and appears in the Book of Common Prayer as a day of fasting and humiliation. Five churches are named after him.

Childe Roland (F) He rescued his sister, Burd Ellen, who was trapped in the Underworld by its king, with the help of *Merlin*. [94, 144]

Chough (B) The Cornish chough is believed to be the form in which *Arthur* exists, prior to his coming again.

Cian mac Cainte (I) Father of *Lugh*. When he encountered the sons of *Tuirenn* — *Brian*, *Iuchar* and *Iucharba* — his enemies approaching, he turned himself into a *pig*. Brian noticed that it was a magical beast and turned himself and his brothers into hounds and gave chase to it. They eventually resumed their own forms, but refused Cian quarter, stoning him to death. They attempted to bury him six times, but only managed to cover him with a mound on the seventh attempt. Lugh found his father's body with the help of the men of the *sidhe*, and vowed vengeance on his killers.

Later legend saw him as an evil druid who enjoyed changing his pupils into *hares*, while he followed as a hound. The children of Tuirenn struck him with his own staff and turned him into a *boar*, whence the earthwork dividing North and South Ireland is called the Black Pig's Dyke, after his tremendous career from coast to coast. This legend corresponds to that of *Twrch Trwyth*. [13, 80, 99]

Cigfa (W) Wife of *Pryderi*, daughter of Gwyn Gohoyw, of the royal line of Casnar Wledig. After her husband and mother-in-law, *Rhiannon*, were spirited away into the Otherworld, she was left alone with her father-in-law, *Manawyddan* with whom she lived until the enchantments lying upon Dyfed were lifted. [17, 80]

Clarisant/Clarisse (A) According to a single Arthurian romance she was the sister of *Gawain*, who lived in a magic castle. *Perceval* overcomes her lover *Guireomelant* in the same text, 'Sir Percevelle'. Nowhere else is Gawain said to have a sister, but this is interesting as it brings the number of the Orkney clan up to five — the others being *Gaheris*, *Gareth* and *Agravaine*. As a Goddess-figure, their mother, *Morgause* of Orkney, should by rights have given birth to this number of children. [190]

Clas Myrddyn (A) *Merlin*'s enclosure. The ancient British tradition that Britain itself was watched over by Merlin as its guardian. Esoterically, Merlin's imprisonment by *Nimue* has its basis in Clas Myrddyn — the place where Merlin is willingly confined in order to watch over its fortunes. [28, 80]

Clim of the Clough (L) See *Adam Bell* and *William of Cloudesley*.

Cocidius (C) A Northern war-god often associated by the Romans with *Mars*. He is depicted as a stylized Celtic warrior with spear and shield. [103, 119]

Cock (B) The cock has ever been the bird of dawning whose call dispels the horrors of the night. Numerous folk-songs and stories attest to this understanding, and in many night-visiting songs where by a dead lover comes to his woman's bed by night, his ghost is dispelled by the cock crowing.

Coinchend (I) The wife of *Morgan*, king of the Land of Wonders. She was the mother of *Delbchaem*, whom she kept guarded because of a prophecy that said on the marriage of her daughter, she herself would die. She kept the girl in a fortress palisaded with stakes upon each of which was the head an unsuccessful suitor. She fought *Art* but was beheaded by him. This story corresponds to *Gereint*'s adventure in Joy of the Court episode. [6, 99]

Colgrevance (A) Knight of the *Round Table* who first encountered the Adventure of the magic fountain in *Broceliande*. When water was poured from a basin over an emerald stone at its brim, a black knight appeared with a challenge. Colgrevance was defeated, though he managed to escape and it was his story which awakened the interest of *Owain*, who was successful and himself became guardian of the fountain for a time. Colgrevance is said to have been later killed by *Lancelot* while the latter was making his escape from the Queen's chamber. [20]

Collen (ST) The medieval legend makes him an opponent of *Gwynn ap Nudd*, Lord of the Underworld, whom he overcame at *Glastonbury* Tor.

Columba/Columcille (ST) (c.521–97) He was born in Donegal of the royal Ui Neill line and was trained as a monk under Saint Finnian of Moville. He borrowed a copy of Jerome's new translations of the Psalms from the Magh Bile monastery in order to copy it. The original owners judged that the copy should remain with them since 'every cow has its calf'. The resulting battle at Cooldrebhne saw Columba as an opponent in arms, rather than in Christian temperance, and he sent himself into exile from Ireland, in remorse.

He converted many of the Irish settlers in Scotland, as well as King Brude of the Picts. He founded his monastery on Iona which became in time the burial place and assembly of Scottish kings. Many monastic settlements sprang from the influence of Iona. Columba, although he swore never to see Ireland again, returned to champion the social obligations of the Irish in Scotland to the Irish High Kings. He also arbitrated between the Church and the bards, whose position was seriously endangered: Irish poets had become feared and hated due to their practice of satirizing ungenerous patrons (considered in its magical light, since satires could cause physical effects) and because of their extortionate retainers. Columba was himself a poet and his arbitration ensured that Irish poets should be allowed to exercise their ancient function. He is remembered on 9 June.

Conaire Mess Buachalla (I) Grandson of *Etain*, son of *Mess Buachalla*. He was proclaimed King of Tara after he had been prophesied by a druid. He was given a great many geasa (prohibitions) by his otherworldly father such as not sleeping in a house from which firelight could be seen after sun-set. His foster brothers, jealous of his success, conspired to bring him to Da Derga's hostel, where Conaire was compelled to break each of his geasa. He was there attacked and betrayed and although his champion, Mac Cecht fought valiantly to defend him, he died. Only *Conall Cernach* escaped. [6]

Conall Cernach (I) Conall the Victorious preceded *CuChulainn* as the great hero of the Red Branch Warriors in Ulster. He was the only survivor of the destruction of Da Derga's hostel, where *Conaire* was killed. With *Loegaire*, he appears as CuChulainn's rival in the story of *Bricriu*'s Feast where the three heroes contended for the hero's portion of the feast and were challenged by *Cu Roi mac Daire* to the *beheading game*. [6, 12]

Conan Maol (I) One of the *Fianna*. Like *Bricriu* of the Red Branch Knights and *Kay* of the *Round Table Knights*, Conan was the thorn in the side of his fellows, yet he performed many reckless deeds in their honour. He mounted the *horse* of the *Giolla Deacair*, and went to *Tir na Tairngire* until he was rescued by *Fionn*. [8, 13, 21]

Conchobar mac Nessa (I) Son of *Nessa* and *Cathbad*. He was born on the same day as Christ. Nessa won for him the right to be King of Ulster from *Fergus mac Roigh*. He was uncle of *CuChulainn*. He wished to marry his ward, *Deirdriu*, but when she fled with *Naoisi* and his brothers to Alba he gave chase. Although he promised to forgive them, he killed Deirdriu's abductors and slept with her. A sling-shot was lodged in his brain which surgeons could not remove lest he die. On hearing of the crucifixion of Christ he over-exerted himself trying to avenge him, the sling-shot then fell out of his head and he died. [6, 54]

Conganchas mac Daire (I) The brother of *Cu Roi*. He was one of three plagues which *Celtchair* was obligated to overcome, for Conganchas ravaged the land and was invulnerable to ordinary weapons. Celtchair made his daughter, *Niamh*, marry this man so that she might discover how to overcome him. She learned that he was vulnerable in the soles of his feet and calves of his legs, into which sharp spears could be stuck, and so Celtchair killed him. This tale is clearly related to the British *Grail* story of *Peredur*. [182]

Conlaoch (I) Son of *Aoife* and *CuChulainn*. His father left him a ring and bade Aoife send him to her when he was old enough to bear arms. She laid three geasa upon him: not to refuse a challenge, never to give way to anyone, and never to tell his name. When he landed in Ireland he met and was challenged by CuChulainn. Although he knew his father and could have killed him easily, Conlaoch missed the mortal blow and was killed by his father. CuChulainn then saw the ring and realized whom he had slain. [12]

Conn Cetchathach (I) Conn of the Hundred Battles. Husband of *Becuma*. He agreed to the banishment of *Art*, his son by a former marriage. The year of his union with Becuma caused Ireland to become a *wasteland*, without corn or milk. His druids said that the land could only be healed through the bloodshed of a boy of sinless parents. He went on a quest for such a boy, leaving the kingdom to Art in his absence. Conn travelled to the Otherworld, and begged that the beautiful youth called *Segda Saerlabraid* be allowed to come to Ireland and be bathed in waters which would heal the land. Segda realized what was intended but he was willing to die.

Just then a lowing *cow* and a wailing woman appeared (see *Rigru Roisclethan*). She asked the druids what was in the bags on the cow's back. They could not tell her. She judged that the cow should be killed in place of the youth and that the bags be opened. They revealed a bird with one leg and a bird with twelve legs. The birds contended, and the woman revealed that the druids were the twelve-legged one who lost the combat, and Segda was the one-legged one. She then called on Conn to execute his druids for false judgement and to put away Becuma. Conn also discovered, by accident, the Stone of Fal (see *Hallows*) which screamed under the feet of a rightful king, the same number of times as he would have reigning heirs. When the druid would not tell him who they would be, Conn had a vision of *Sovereignty* with her cup of gold and *Lugh* who told him the number of kings to succeed him. [6, 54, 99, 186]

Conn mac Lir (I) He was the son of *Aobh*. He was turned into a swan by his stepmother, *Aoife*.

Connla (I) One of the *Fianna*. He fell in love with a woman from *Tir na mBeo*.

Corbenic (A) The castle of the *Grail Kings*. The name possibly derives from the words 'Corps Benit' (Blessed Body), and has been seen as one of the riddles of the *Grail*. [83]

Corc (I) He was born Conall mac Luigthig and was fostered by a witch, *Fedelm*. During a ritual, his ear became magically singed and so he was called Corc or red. He was fostered by *Crimthann*, his cousin, who sent Corc to the King of the Picts with a secret ogham message on his shield, implying that the King kill the bearer. However, a scholar, whom Corc had rescued from slavery, altered the characters so that they bore a favourable meaning. Corc was welcomed and married the Pictish king's daughter. He returned home after his cousin's death and founded a dynasty of his own at Femhen. Shortly afterwards he discovered the site of his descendant's royal fortress, Cashel. Beleaguered in a snowstorm, he beheld a vision of a yew-bush growing over a stone and angels going up and down before it. His druids told him that whoever kindled a fire on that stone should be king of Munster forever. So Corc founded the dynasty of the Munster Eoghanacht or People of the Yew.

Cordelia (L) Youngest daughter of King *Lear*. She refused to flatter her father and was wed to Aganippus, King of the Franks, without a dowry. She later received her father when he had been beggared and outcast by her elder sisters Goneril and Regan. She became Queen of Britain after his death. In earliest Celtic legend she is *Creuddylad*, daughter of *Llyr*. Her sisters' husbands captured her and she committed suicide in prison. Her story is similar to the folk-heroine, Cap-O-Rushes. Shakespeare reworked the legend in 'King Lear'. [9]

Corineus (L) He accompanied *Brutus* as leader of the second group of Trojans. He was given Cornwall as his province and wrestled with the giant *Gogmagog*. [9]

Cormac Cond Longes (I) The son of *Conchobar mac Nessa*. He was exiled because his championship of *Fergus mac Roigh* at the treachery of Conchobar's slaying of the sons of *Usna*. As Conchobar lay dying, he asked his son to return and become king. Despite a prophecy warning of the possible outcome, Cormac went. During his stay at a hostel, *Craiftine* played his harp so soothingly that Cormac slept and was overpowered by soldiers. [182]

Cormac mac Art (I) Son of *Art* and grandson of *Conn Cetchathach*. He was stolen by a she-wolf and raised as one of her cubs. He was recognized as Art's son because of his perceptive judgements in a case of litigation. He restored Tara to its former greatness. He visited *Tir Tairngire* where he was given the silver branch of *Manannan*.

While there he encountered the cup of truth. If three falsehoods were said over it it broke, but if three truths were said over it it reunited. He was the father of *Grainne*, wife of *Finn mac Cumhail*, whom he appointed chief of his warband or *Fianna*. He died choking on a salmon-bone. He is credited with being an early Christian, refusing burial at the usual cemetery of Bruig na Boinne, but being buried upright with his face to the East. His great wisdom caused him to be called the Irish Solomon. [5, 6]

Coventina (C) A river-goddess whose cult was centred upon the temple at Carrawburgh, Northumberland. A relief depicts the triple goddess, each aspect holding up a jar of water in one hand and pouring out water with the other. Local springs were held in reverence as natural foci of divine energy. [60, 103]

Co-walker (S) Robert Kirk described these beings in his 'Secret Commonwealth' as 'a twin-brother and companion, in every way like (a) man, haunting him as his shadow. . .both before and after the Original is dead.' A kind of doppelgänger. [71]

Cow (B) So central to the economy of Britain and Ireland was the cow in early times that it was considered a unit of currency. In Ireland, for instance, a slave-woman was worth three cows. Lords were called 'bo-aire' or cow-lord. Until the last two hundred years, drovers' roads were the main routes across country and, anciently, the two halves of the Celtic year were determined by the movement of cattle: *Beltaine* marking their coming into summer pasture and *Samhain* being the time when winter-slaughter of cattle was undertaken, to lay down stocks of meat against the long cold time and to conserve the strength of the herd. The cow was considered to be under the special protection of Saint *Brigit*, who was invoked to keep the beasts in good health and to promote their milk-yield and fertility. The bleached hide of cows made the vellum upon which the very stories in this present book were originally recorded by clerics. The cow is also under the protection of Saint *Columba* who would, however, not allow any on Iona because 'where a cow is, there a woman is also, and where a woman is, trouble follows.' [183]

Cradelmass (A) King of Norgalles (North Wales) in *Arthur*'s time, he was one of the rebel kings whom Arthur defeated at the beginning of his reign. As the grandson of King *Ryons*, it is perhaps not surprising that he is an unpleasant character.

Craiftine (I) He was harper to *Labraid Longseach*. He gained his harp due to a peculiarity of his master's, for Labraid had horse-ears. This blemish was kept secret from everyone lest Labraid be deposed, but his barber knew and he was sworn to secrecy. However, he could not restrain himself from telling a tree. This was cut down and made into a harp for Craiftine but when it was played, it revealed the truth about the King. Craiftine also harped the parents of *Moriath* to sleep so that Labraid could love her. *Cormac Cond Longes* slept with Craiftine's wife, to revenge which, Craiftine was a party to Cormac's death, again by lulling him asleep. [182]

Crane (I) The crane is no longer native to Britain, but there is a strong Celtic tradition that cranes are people transmogrified into bird-shape, possibly for a penance. Saint *Columba* turned a queen and his handmaid into cranes as a punishment. One of the wonders of Ireland was supposed to be a crane which lived on the island of Inis-Kea, Co. Mayo; it has been there since the beginning of the world and will live there until the day of judgement. The imperturbable patience of the crane has perhaps lent verisimilitude to this story. Generally, the crane was associated with the *Cailleach*, and was a secret, magical bird. Its skin went to make *Manannan's Cranebag*. [103, 183]

Crane Bag (I) This receptacle for the ancient *Hallows* of Ireland was owned by *Manannan mac Lir*. It was formed from the skin of *Aoife*, Manannan's son's mistress, who had been changed into a crane because of her jealous behaviour. In it were kept Manannan's house, shirt, knife, the belt and smith's hook of *Goibniu*, the shears of the King of Alba, the helmet of the King of Lochlann, the belt of fish-skin, and the bones of Asal's *pig* which the son of *Tuirenn* had been sent to fetch by *Lugh*. The treasures were only visible at high-tide, at the ebb-tide they would vanish. The bag was passed from Manannan to Lugh, then to Cumhal and finally to *Fionn*. The contents of the crane's bag correspond to the Hallows of *Annwn* and to the treasures guarded by *Twrch Trwyth*. [13]

Credne (I) He helped forge the weapons for the *Tuatha de Danaan*. He was a worker in bronze. He assisted *Diancecht* in making *Nuadu*'s silver hand and arm. [5]

Creiddylad (W) Daughter of *Lludd Llaw Ereint*. She eloped with *Gwythyr ap Greidawl*, but was abducted by *Gwynn ap Nudd* before he could sleep with her. *Arthur* judged that neither man should have her and that each should fight for her every May Day until Judgement Day: whoever won on that occasion would be the winner. This ancient motif recalls the mystery drama of the Winter and Summer combat for the hand of the Flower Maiden, or Spring. This theme is also preserved within the story of *Tristan, Isolt* and King *Mark*. [17, 28, 80]

Creidne (I) She was a woman warrior within the *Fianna*, having fled from home where her father had begotten three sons upon her.

Creirwy (W) Daughter of *Ceridwen* and *Tegid Foel*. The Triads cite her as one of the three fair maidens of Britain. [17, 80]

Crimthann (I) He was the cousin of *Corc* and also his foster-father. After Crimthann's wife complained, unjustly, of Corc's attentions to her, he sent his cousin to the King of the Picts with ogham inscriptions on his shield which only the Pictish King could read — they indicated that the bearer should be slain. However, Crimthann soon died and Corc returned home to the kingship.

Crodhmara (S) These are fairy cattle which give three times the amount of milk of an ordinary beast.

Crom Cruach (I) The gold and silver image to which the Irish offered their first fruits and first-born in pagan times. It stood on the plain of Mag Slecht in Ulster. It bent down to Saint *Patrick* and was overcome, sinking back into the earth.

Cronos (G) Greek Cronos ate his children by Rhea — all except Zeus who escaped this fate and caused Cronos to regurgitate his siblings. He then punished his father by chaining him whilst asleep and imprisoning him on the island of *Ogygia*. Cronos is the ruler of the Golden Age — a period of everlasting joy. This legend has been amalgamated with those concerning British traditions of the *Blessed Islands* of the West, wherein the Golden Age and the earthly paradise combine to make a place of otherworldly peace. Cronos' legend runs as an undercurrent through the career of *Bran* who rules over a similar otherworldly realm. [35, 57, 80]

Crow (B) Like the *raven*, crow is primarily associated with battle and death. The Irish for 'crow' is 'badh', a name given to one of the battle-goddesses associated with the *Morrighan*. The crow exemplifies the function of assimilation and reintegration within the mythic structure. [185]

Crudel (A) Pagan king of Britain who threw *Joseph of Arimathea* and his followers into prison, where they were sustained by the power of the *Grail*. The captives were ultimately released by *Mordrains* and *Seraphe*, who had converted to Christianity and become followers of the Grail.

Crunnchu mac Agnoman (I) The husband of *Macha* who foolishly boasted his wife's prowess and speed in the hearing of the king. She expired after having beaten the king's race-horse, cursing Ulster with her last breath. [5, 27]

Crystabell (L) Daughter of Sir Prinsamour in the romance of 'Sir Eglamour of Artoys'. Her complex story includes a series of escapes and misunderstandings in which she first loses her lover *Eglamour*, then her son, who is stolen by a griffin. Later she accidentally marries her own offspring, only to discover her mistake in time to find Eglamour and marry him!

Cu Roi mac Daire (I) A king of Munster with great otherworldly powers. He appropriated many otherwordly *Hallows* which the Ulstermen had captured, including his wife, *Blanaid*, loved by *CuChulainn*. She deceived him and enabled CuChulainn to kill him. Cu Roi disguised himself as the *Wild Herdsman* and challenged the heroes of Ulster to play the *Beheading Game* with him. He is the

Celtic prototype of the Green Knight. His death was avenged by Lugaid, his son. [5, 12, 76, 80]

Cu Sith (S) The fairy dog which was usually green in colour and the size of a young bullock. It was normally only recognized by its great pawprints after it had passed by in mud or snow, but if encountered was extremely dangerous.

CuChulainn (I) Hero of the Red Branch Knights of Ulster. He was the son of Dechtire and Lugh. His birth name was Setanta but he gained his adult name after killing the fierce hound of Conchobar's smith, Culainn. In recompense for the loss, Setanta agreed to guard Culainn's forge until a suitable dog could be found, and so he became Cu Chulainn (Hound of Culainn). He was fostered and trained by the best men in Ulster. He wooed Emer, but her father would not accept him until he had trained with Scathach of Alba. He fought her rival, Aoife and lay with her engendering his only son, Conlaoch, whom he later killed unknowingly. He was famed for his great skills: the salmon-leap, which enabled him to leap over obstacles, and his use of the gae-bolg, the great spear which inflicted the death-blow. (This weapon corresponds to the spear of Lugh, his father, whom he represents in mortal realms.)

He accepted the challenge of the club-carrying giant (Cu Roi mac Daire, in disguise) to the Beheading Game at Bricriu's Feast at which he was proclaimed supreme champion of Ulster. He later killed Cu Roi mac Daire who had humiliated him by shaving CuChulainn's head, with the help of Blanaid. He defended Ulster single-handed at the ford when Maeve of Connacht came against them: Ulster's warriors were prostrate and enfeebled by the curse of Macha. Only CuChulainn (who was not a native Ulsterman) was able to fight on their behalf. He accepted many single-combats, slaying all comers until Maeve sent his old friend and fellow-pupil, Ferdiad, whom he reluctantly killed. He was finally overcome by Lugaid, son of Cu Roi mac Daire, with the help of the daughters of Calatin.

He bound himself upright to a pillar-stone in order to face the imaginary host which had been conjured up by his opponents. His death was avenged by Conall Cernach. CuChulainn's battle-frenzy was renowned: his body contorted itself horribly, blood spurted from his head in a great gush and his anger was unquenchable unless a host of women were sent out naked to meet his chariot. His sword was Cruaidin Cailidcheann (Hard-Headed). His two horses which yoked his chariot were called Liath Macha and Dubh Sanglainn. CuChulainn loved many women apart from his wife, but he refused the love of the Morrighan who became his implacable enemy, causing him to forsake his geasa. His adventures and exploits can only be suggested in this entry. He corresponds to Conchobar as Gawain does to Arthur. [5, 12, 27, 160]

Cuimhne (I) She was a *cailleach* who assisted *Mongan* to retrieve his wife, *Dub Lacha* from *Brandubh*. She magically changed into a beautiful woman so that Brandubh was willing to exchange Dubh Lacha for her. After Mongan and his wife had gone, she resumed her normal hag-like appearance. This is one of the only instances when the transformatory hag after having become beautiful resumes her former shape, although this is threatened by *Ragnell* in the *Gawain* and Ragnell story. [182]

Cuirithir (I) He was a poet who loved *Liadin*. When she refused to marry him and became a nun, he became a monk. He was exiled from Ireland after which Liadin died of grief.

Culhwch (W) Son of Celyddon Wledig, nephew of *Arthur*. His mother, *Goleuddydd*, bore him after having been terrified by the sight of pigs, so that he was called Culhwch or Pig-Sty. His father remarried on the death of Goleuddydd. Culhwch's stepmother laid a gease upon Culhwch that he should marry none other than *Olwen*, the daughter of *Yspaddaden Pencawr*, the giant. He went to *Arthur*'s court and there demanded, in the names of all present, that his uncle help him procure Olwen.

At the court of Yspaddaden, Culhwch was given thirty-nine 'anoethu' or impossible tasks, which must be fulfilled before he can marry Olwen, all of which are performed with the help of Arthur's court. The chief task was to hunt the *Twrch Trwyth*, a giant *boar*, for which are required many particular *horses*, hounds and men, including *Mabon*, the wondrous youth, whose finding is narrated in this story. Other tasks include the voyage of Arthur to the Underworld in order to obtain some of the *Hallows* or *Thirteen Treasures of Britain* — a feat which is likewise related in a ninth-century Welsh poem, the Preiddu Annwn. Yspaddaden's power is overthrown and Culhwch marries Olwen. (See *Hallows*.) [17, 28, 72, 76, 80]

Cundrie/Kundrie (A) The name, in *Parzival*, of the *Loathly Lady* who also mocks and helps the *Grail Knight* on his quest. She is analogous to *Sovereignty* in her hag-like aspect. [30, 82, 83]

Custennin (W) The giant herdsman who guards the flocks of *Yspaddaden Pencawr*, who deprived him of his living and inhabited his lands. His twenty-four sons were all destroyed by the giant, except *Goreu*, whom his mother hid in a cupboard. He aids *Culhwch* and his compantions to defeat Yspaddaden, although it is Goreu who eventually avenges his father. [17, 80]

Cuthbert (ST) (634–87) He became a monk of the Celtic Church after receiving a vision of Saint *Aidan*'s spirit ascending to heaven. After the synod of Whitby (see Saint Hilda), when Celtic customs were brought into line with the universal church of Rome, he accepted the reformations and became Prior of Lindisfarne. He was a life-long misogynist. A legend tells that he had been falsely accused of fathering a child and he swore never to allow a woman to approach him again. There is still in Durham Cathedral, where he is buried, a line supposedly demarking the portion of the church forbidden to women. His love of animals offsets this attitude. His long hours of prayer standing upright in the sea were relieved by the breath of *seals* who dried him after his labours. His feast-day is 20 March.

Cwn Annwn (W) Like the *Gabriel Hounds* which run in the *Wild Hunt*, the Cwn Annwn (Hounds of *Annwn*) were much feared as death-portents. They are known by their distinctive belling which starts like that of a beagle and, when near, sounds more like a blood-hound. They are usually white with red-tipped ears. *Pwyll* encountered them when he met *Arawn*'s hunt.

Cyhyreath (W) The Welsh form of the *Caoineag*. Her crying sounds like that of the groans of the dying. Although she is usually invisible, her presence is sometimes noticed by the appearance of corpse-candles.

Cymbeline (L) King of Britain, trained in the household of Augustus Caesar. He handed over his kingdom to his son, Guidarius, who refused to pay tribute to the Romans. Behind the legend stands the historical Cunobeline, a minor British king. Shakespeare, drawing upon Holinshed's 'Chronicles', wrote a play, 'Cymbeline', in which many minor traditions of British mythology are incorporated. [9]

D

Drake's Drum

Dagda (I) One of the *Tuatha de Danaan*. *Bres* ordered him to build forts but would give him little food. Together with *Lugh* and *Ogma*, he planned to attack the *Fomorians*. He mated with the *Morrighan* over a river and she prophesied his success. Attired as a rustic fool, he entered the enemy stronghold where he discovered the disposition of the Fomorians. His harp was called 'the Oak of Two Greens' and 'the Four-Angled Music'. With it he was able to play three kinds of music: the sorrow-strain, the laugh-strain and the sleep-strain. It was with the latter that he was able to subdue those Fomorians who had abducted his harper. He was the guardian of the *cauldron* which satisfied all hunger, brought from *Murias*. (See *Hallows*.) His name means 'Good God', but his other names or titles are Eochaid Ollathair (All-Father) and Ruad Rofessa (Lord of Great Knowledge) indicating his similarity to the *Wild Herdsman*. [5, 15, 99]

Dagonet (A) King *Arthur*'s jester who is made a knight as a joke and later shows his bravery in several tournaments. His wit and unorthodox behaviour enliven the more tedious passages of Malory's Book of *Tristan*.

Daireann (I) Daughter of *Bobh Dearg* who desired *Fionn* to become her husband with her as sole wife for one year. When he refused, she gave him poison so that in his madness the *Fianna* deserted him. It was Daireann's sister, *Sadbh* who became the mother of *Oisin*.

Dame du Lac (A) See *Lady of the Lake*.

Danu (I) The ancestress of the *Tuatha de Danaan*. So antique is her legend that no stories have survived. She is analogous with *Anu*, and may survive in *Black Annis*. [99]

Daoine Sidhe (I) The people of the *Sidhe* or hollow hills. The inhabitants of the Otherworld who, like the *Fairies*, live behind the world of men but sometimes co-exist peacefully with them. There is a long tradition that the ancient gods and heroes entered the sidhe and lived there. As with other inner-world peoples, they are referred to euphemistically as 'the Gentry' or the 'Good People'. (See *Aes Sidhe*.) [55]

David/Dewi (ST) (d.601) The patron of Wales. He was born in Cardiganshire and founded twelve monasteries from Croyland to Pembrokeshire, where the regime was particularly austere, after the Celtic fashion. He was nicknamed 'Aquaticus' after his habit of only drinking water. Although Welshmen remember him on 1 March with leeks, his actual emblem is the dove. [91]

Dechtire (I) Sister of *Conchobar*. She and her fifty attendant maidens disappeared for three years. She was discovered, in bird-form, in a house of the *Sidhe* by *Bricriu* who concealed this from Conchobar — he merely told the king that he had been royally entertained in that place. Conchobar sent a message to the sidhe demanding that the woman of the house be sent to him, in order that he might sleep with her, according to the kingly rights. She was sent but was in labour on arrival. In the morning she bore a son and Bricriu at last revealed that the woman was Dechtire. The father was *Lugh*, and the child was called *Setanta* until he killed the hound of Culann the Smith when he was afterwards called *CuChulainn*. [5, 12]

Deer (B) The deer is one of the foremost transformatory beasts in British mythology, especially in its form of the White Doe or White Stag, which is frequently an otherworldly messenger which hunters encounter, leading them ever deeper into the forest to unknown wonders. From the White Stag encountered by *Pwyll* to the White Hart which *Galahad* sees, betokening Christ, pagan and folklore traditions have asserted the beauty and mystical grace of this creature. *Sadbh* was enchanted into the form of a doe, *Gilfaethwy*, while *Gwydion* was changed into a stag. The human antlered figure has been a potent image from primeval times onwards, from the shaman-hunter and the *Wild Herdsman* in his form of *Cernunnos*, to the Abbots Bromley Horn Dance which is still danced every September — the time when the deer are in rut. [80, 81]

Degrabel (L) Son of *Eglamour* and *Crystabell* who was stolen away by a griffin and brought up by the King of Israel. He subsequently married his mother but discovered his mistake in time and the marriage was dissolved. Later he fell in love with and married Ardanata.

Deirdriu/Deirdre (I) Daughter of Fedlimid, harper of *Conchobar*. *Cathbad* prophesied that she would bring death and sorrow to Ulster and, though the Ulstermen demanded her death, Conchobar fostered her secretly with *Lebharcham* until Deirdriu was old enough to be his wife. Deirdriu saw some *ravens* feasting on blood in the snow and wished for a man whose skin was as white as the snow, whose hair as black as the raven's, and whose cheek would be as red as the blood.

She met *Naoisi* and put a *gease* on him to take her away with him. With Naoisi and his brothers, she wandered throughout Ireland, pursued by Conchobar, until they fled to Alba at last. *Fergus mac Roigh* was sent to fetch them back, promising Conchobar's friendship, but they were betrayed on their return. The sons of *Usnach* were slain and Deirdriu was bound to Conchobar as his wife. He eventually gave her to Eoghan, a client king, who had dealt the death blow to Naoisi. Between these twin evils she flung herself from Eoghan's chariot and dashed her brains out on a stone. Her laments for the life she had lived in Alba contain the purest strain of poetic lament in Irish literature. Like Helen of Troy, Deirdriu ushers in the decline of Ulster's greatness. [12, 160]

Delbchaem (I) The daughter of *Morgan*, king of the land of wonders and of *Coinchend*. She could not be won by any man because of a prophecy that when she married, her mother would die. She was kept secluded and guarded by monsters, hags and hostile terrain — all of which *Art* surmounted in order to win her. [6]

Demne (I) The childhood name which *Fionn* took when he was tutored by *Finneces*. [104]

Derfel (ST) Sometimes called Derfel Cadarn (the Strong). Very little is known about him, except that his legend calls him a warrior who distinguished himself at the Battle of *Camlan*. He was the founder and patron of Llanderfel in Gwynedd, where a wooden statue of him on a horse, holding a staff, was shown. During the Reformation this image was burned at Smithfield along with Katherine of Aragon's confessor, Friar John Forest, because there was a prophecy saying that the image would one day set a forest on fire. Derfel is remembered on 5 April.

Devorgilla (I) She was to be given in tribute to the *Fomorians* but was rescued by *CuChulainn* who offered her in marriage to *Lugaid*. Angry at this slight she attempted to kill CuChulainn. He wounded and then healed her by sucking her blood. By this action they became blood brother and sister.

Diana (RB) Dedications to Diana occur throughout Britain, including one temple which was re-dedicated on an old Iron-age site at Maiden Castle, denoting perhaps a native cult of a similar, unnamed goddess. She was the goddess of venery and it is in this aspect that she is natively recognized. The site of St Paul's Cathedral, London, was anciently sacred to her and there is a tradition that live bucks were processed up its steps until medieval times. [59, 119]

Diancecht (I) Grandfather of *Lugh*. He was the physician of the *Tuatha de Danaan*. Assisted by *Credne*, he made the silver hand to replace the one lost by *Nuadu* in battle. The mortally wounded Tuatha were bathed in the well, Slane, which he had specially blessed by him, recovering to fight on. (See *Cauldron*.) [5]

Diarmuid (I) Hero of the *Fianna*. Nephew of Fionn. He was fostered in the *Sidhe* of Bruig na Boinne by *Angus Og*. His father, Donn, accidentally killed the Steward's son in that place. The Steward struck his son with a wand and turned him into a wild boar, charging him to kill Donn's son when the time came, on which account Diarmuid was forbidden to hunt that boar. He had a love-spot, making him irresistible to women. *Grainne* put a *gease* on him to run away with her when she saw the ageing Fionn who had come to woo her.

They ran away together but had no rest, since Fionn swore that they should not sleep under one roof on two consecutive nights, nor eat a meal in the same place twice. After a long pursuit, Fionn made peace with them, but he sent Diarmuid to hunt the boar which wounded him. He begged a healing drink from Fionn's hands, but such was Fionn's jealousy and anger that the water dripped from his fingers to the ground and Diarmuid died. This story is a direct parallel to that of *Tristan* and *Isolt*, or *Lancelot* and *Guinevere*. [13, 159]

Dinadan (A) Knight of the *Round Table*. Apart from *Dagonet*, he is about the only figure in the Arthurian sagas who has a genuine sense of humour and no little satirical talent. He wrote a lampoon against King *Mark*, and in a tournament in which *Lancelot* took part played all kinds of pranks on the other knights. Lancelot, in the spirit of the event, appeared in the lists wearing a dress over his armour and having overcome Dinadan carried him into the woods and dressed him as a woman. He was later, sadly, killed by *Mordred* and his henchmen.

Dinas Emrys (A) A hill in North Wales believed to be the site of *Vortigern*'s Tower. Every time the masons tried to erect the tower it fell down and Vortigern caused his druids to discover why. They advised the killing of a boy whose blood could caulk the foundations. *Merlin* was brought, as a boy, and told Vortigern that the reason was that two dragons lay beneath the site in a stone chest, continually fighting. These represented the two nations of the British and the Saxons, to whom Vortigern had sold his kingship.

Dindrane (A) The name sometimes given to *Perceval*'s sister. She gave her blood willingly to heal a woman suffering from leprosy and her body accompanied the *Grail Knights* on the Ship of Solomon to *Sarras*.

Diuran (I) He was one of *Maelduine*'s companions on the immrama (wonder voyages).

Diwrnach/Dyrnwch (W) The possessor of a magical *cauldron* which would not boil the food of a coward. He is variously described as the steward of the King of Ireland and also as a giant. The finding of this cauldron is the subject of the early Welsh poem, the 'Preiddeu Annwn', and is also described in 'Culhwch and Olwen'. [17, 28, 80]

Dog (B) The dog or hound has ever been a faithful servant of humanity and this is reflected in British myth and folklore where the dog is frequently one of the helping animals of the hero's search. *Arthur's Cabal* is one such dog, and *Fionn*'s Bran and Sceolan are others. The hounds of the Otherworld or Underworld are always white with red-tipped ears, and these are the pack which ride with the *Wild Hunt*. *CuChulainn* was named after he overcame Culainn's hound and it was geise for him to eat dog's flesh — a proscription he broke just before his death, since it was also his geise never to refuse hospitality offered to him: the *Morrighan* invited him to eat of a roasted dog.

Dolorous Blow (A) The blow accidentally struck by *Balin* which wounded the *Grail King*, *Pelles*, and caused the *Wasteland*. [20, 83]

Don (W) The mother of the Welsh pantheon as projected within the four branches of the 'Mabinogion'. She has been associated with the Irish *Danu*. Her life and deeds are unrecorded, so antique is her origin. She represents the Celtic *Magna Mater* as the mother of the sacred tribe, the genetrix of all peoples. In star-lore she is remembered in the constellation, as Llys Don, or Casseopeia. [17, 99]

Donn (I) Donn was the Lord of the Dead. His house, Tech Duinn, was located on one of the islands off south-west Munster. It is here that the dead gather prior to their Otherworld journey to the Isles of the Blest.

Donn Cuailgne (I) The Brown *Bull* of Cuailgne was owned by *Daire* and became the object of much strife. He was the eternal enemy of a swineherd; both of them went through time in different shapes

— animals, *dragons*, demons and birds — until the Cattle Raid of Cooley, when his rival was the White Bull of Connacht. The two bulls killed each other in combat.

Dragon (B) The dragon appears in much more than its classical forms within British mythology. It is sometimes a *worm* and is derived from northern European prototypes. It is sometimes a water-serpent or monster. In all instances, the dragon exemplifies elemental power, especially of the earth. The dragon which Saint *George* overcomes is symbolic of paganism, but such obvious symbolism overlays a great deal more subtle imagery. The two dragons which *Merlin* Emrys releases from under *Vortigern*'s tower are emblematic of the vitality of the land which is chaotic unless tamed or wielded by a true ruler. In a story about the origin of *Samhain* Eve we read that the dragon is symbolic of the *Cailleach* who holds the power of winter over *Brigit*'s lamb, symbolic of spring. [110, 186]

Drake, Sir Francis (1540–96) The first circumnavigator of the world who fought against the Spanish Armada, he has passed into legend as a hero possessed of supernatural powers. The Spanish called him El Draco (The Dragon), and the luck which attended his daring exploits certainly pointed to special guidance. The drum which accompanied him on his circumnavigation is kept at Buckland Abbey; it can be heard beating when England is endangered. Moreover, Drake is supposed to be only sleeping, like *Arthur*, and will rise at his country's need.

Drustan (A) See *Tristan*.

Dubh (I) She was a druidess who, on discovering that her husband had another wife, drowned her rival. Her husband then cast at her with his sling and she fell into a pool which was called Dubhlinn or Dublin. The Romans called it Nigratherma — literally Black Pool, but perhaps a more ancient name for Dublin is Baile Atha Cliath or the Town of the Ford of Hurdles.

Dubh Lacha (I) She was the wife of *Mongan*, born on the same night as he. She was loved by *Brandubh*, to whom Mongan was tricked into giving her up. However, with the help of *Cuimhne*, the hag, she was regained.

Dubhlaing (I) He loved *Aoibhell* who prophesied that he would die in battle unless he put on her cloak of invisibility.

Dunstan (ST) (909–88) Abbot of *Glastonbury* and Archbishop of Canterbury. Patron of goldsmiths, jewellers and blacksmiths. Dunstan regularized monastic procedures and codified the present Coronation Rite. He was extremely talented, being able to embroider, paint and play the harp, as well as being a goldsmith and working with other metals. During his making of a golden chalice, he was said to have been assaulted by the devil whom he held fast by the nose with his red-hot tongs. His emblem is still that of a pair of pincers. A treatise on alchemy entitled 'On the Philosopher's Stone' is attributed to him. His feast-day is 19 May.

Dwyn/Donwenna/Dwynwen (ST) (fifth or sixth century) The daughter of King Brychan. A certain Maelon wished to marry her but she rejected him; she dreamt that she was given a drink which delivered her from him but turned Maelon to ice. She then prayed that he be unfrozen, that all lovers should find happiness in each other, or else be cured of love, and that she herself should never marry. She is accordingly the patron of lovers in Wales. Fish were kept at her holy well where she became a nun. They were believed to reveal the destiny of querents at her shrine. She was invoked for the curing of animals. Her feast-day is 25 January.

Dylan (W) Son of *Arianrhod* and brother of *Llew*. He was nicknamed Son of the Wave because he swam off into the sea after being baptized. One of the Triads relates to a lost story concerning his death at the hands of his uncle, *Gofannon*, where it is called one of the Three Unfortunate Blows. [17, 28, 80]

Dympna (ST) (seventh century) The daughter of an Irish king. She looked so like her dead mother that her father conceived an adulterous passion for her, to escape from which she fled with her confessor to Holland. She is patron of the mentally afflicted and is remembered on 15 May.

E

Elen of the Ways

Each Uisge (S) The water-horse which haunts lochs and appears like a sleek pony, offering its back to anyone to be ridden. It then plunges back into the water with its prey. [78]

Eagle (B) The eagle was traditionally considered to be one of the oldest of the animals, as indeed it appears in the search for *Mabon*. *Maelduine* and his companions watch an eagle renewing itself in a secret lake. There are many traditional stories about who can remember the coldest winter's night among the birds. The contest is between the *Hawk* of Achill and the Eagle, who is sent on a fruitless errand, asking all animals until she discovers her chicks have been eaten by the hawk. A Celtic tradition tells that Adam and Eve are believed to be extant in eagle shape. *Fintan* and *Tuan mac Carill* both spend a lifetime in eagle-form, until they finally take residence in the shape of the most long-living and wise animal of all, the *salmon*. [80, 183]

Easal (I) He was the King of the Golden Pillars whose seven magical *pigs* were endlessly renewed after having been eaten. The finding of these was one of the tasks set by *Lugh* for the Sons of *Tuirenn*.

Eber (I) Son of *Miled*. He unsuccessfully fought his brother *Eremon* for the kingship of Ireland.

Ector de Maris (A) Brother of *Lancelot* and Knight of the *Round Table*. He is sometimes confused with *Ector of the Forest Sauvage*, *Arthur*'s foster-father. [20]

Ector of the Forest Sauvage (A) *Arthur*'s foster-father in Malory. He raised the boy in ignorance of his true family, according to the instruction of *Merlin*. [20, 138]

Edmund (ST) (841–69) King of East Anglia. He led his army against the Danes and was defeated and captured. He was martyred either by being shot full of arrows, or by being spread-eagled after the Viking fashion and offered to their gods. His body was enshrined at Bury St Edmunds where a popular cult grew up about him. His emblem is the arrow and he is remembered on 20 November.

Edward (ST) (962–79) Called 'the Martyr', he was King of England and was assassinated at Corfe Castle by his brother, *Ethelred*'s, retainers. Miracles soon alerted churchmen that his unjust death, though not in defence of the faith, merited greater attention. His youth may well have contributed to his veneration, as did the unholy spilling of royal blood of an anointed sovereign.

Efflam (ST) (sixth century) After an unsuccessful attempt to subdue a serpent, *Arthur* was thirsty. Saint Efflam not only caused a spring to rise but he also defeated the serpent himself. [72]

Efnissien (W) Son of Penarddun by Euroswydd, brother to *Nissien*, the Peaceful. Efnissien, the Unpeaceful, caused much strife between Britain and Ireland. As he was not consulted concerning his half-sister, *Branwen*'s, marriage to *Matholwch*, King of Ireland, he mutilated the Irish horses, causing *Bran* to offer the *cauldron* of rebirth to the Irish in compensation for the insult.

He later averted the certain death of Bran and the British party after they had come to Ireland to rescue Branwen, by murdering 200 Irishmen who were concealed in sacks about the feasting-hall. During the feast of his nephew's accession, Efnissien seized the boy, *Gwern*, and cast him on the fire. In the subsequent combat in which the Irish resuscitated their dead in the life-giving cauldron, Efnissien sacrificed himself to even the odds by stretching himself out in the cauldron. Since it only restored the dead to life and Efnissien was a living man, he was able to burst it asunder and break its power at the cost of his own life.

His extreme behaviour is unreasonable unless it is considered in the light of his role as defender of Britain's *Sovereignty*, which lay in the person of Branwen herself. By marriage to the King of Ireland Branwen brought with her the sovereignty of Britain, which Efnissien sought to avert. [17, 80]

Eglamour (L) A poor knight at the court of Sir Prinsamour who made his castle a centre of Chivalric excellence. Eglamour loved his daughter *Chrystabell* and was told that he could only win her if he achieves three adventures. First he must slay the giant Marrock, then a huge boar who has been ravaging the lands of Prinsamour. His third adventure is to kill a dragon which has been threatening Rome. Eglamour is successful in all his endeavours but meanwhile Chrystabell gives birth to a son and both she and her lover are banished. Her son is stolen by a griffin and Chrystabell herself wanders for years until she again meets up with her lover and their son and all ends happily after many adventures.

Einherier (N) The dead warriors who feasted with *Odin* in *Valhalla*. They were fed by a boar which endlessly replenished itself, and though they fought daily, if killed they were restored to life at the end of the day. In English mythology they are considered to be similar to the *Wild Hunt*.

Elaine de Astolat (A) Sometimes called 'Le Blanke' (White), she was a maiden who fell in love with *Lancelot*. When he failed to return her affection, she was carried down the river to *Camelot* in a boat, bearing a letter, telling of her misfortune. [20]

Elaine of Corbenic (A) Daughter of the *Grail King, Pelles*. Mother of *Galahad*. By sorcery, she became the lover of *Lancelot*. Because she thought he was sleeping with *Guinevere*, Lancelot engendered the child destined to become the Grail-winner by Elaine. She is often confused with *Elaine de Astolat*. [24]

Elaine of Garlot (A) Daughter of *Gorlois* and *Igerna*. She married *Nentres* of Garlot, thus reconciling this enemy king with the newly crowned *Arthur*, her half-brother.

Elatha (I) He was a fair *Fomorian* king whose realm was across the seas. He slept with a daughter of the De Danaan tribe and gave her a ring, prophesying she would bear a son. She gave birth to *Bres* and when he later needed help he redeemed his father's ring by journeying to the Fomorian kingdom and joining them against his mother's clan.

Elcmar (I) Husband of *Boann*. Tradition suggests that he was the original inhabitant and owner of Brugh na Boinne, which was subsequently given to *Angus* in perpetuity, because of his magical power over day and night. [19, 42]

Elen (W) Helen of the Hosts, as she is known in Welsh memory, is the heroine of the story. The 'Dream of Maxen Wledig', who lives in Caernarvon. Maxen dreamt of her, asleep in Rome, and sent messengers to find her. She is credited with the construction and planning of numerous roads in Wales — the Sarnau Helen — some of which are still surviving. Her story and identity were conflated with that of Saint Helena, mother of Constantine the Great. [17, 28, 80, 186]

Elidor (L) Giraldus Cambrensis tells how Elidurus, a priest, had when a boy, been led into *Faery*. He used often to return there until one day, his mother demanded some proof of his visits in the form of a golden ball with which he used to play with the fairies. The way back was barred to him. He remembered their speech, saying that it was much like Greek. Giraldus puts this down to the Britons' descent from *Brutus* and the city of *Troy*. [10]

Ellyllon (W) The Welsh form of *elves*.

Elphin (W) Son of *Gwyddno*. He was the patron of *Taliesin*, whom he discovered in a *salmon* weir on May-Eve. His father had allowed him to draw the annual draught of fish on that night, since Elphin was 'the most unfortunate of youths', not only unlucky but also penniless. When he fished out the leather bag or coracle which contained the boy poet, Elphin cried: 'Behold, the Radiant Brow!' — thus naming Taliesin.

The poet consoled his patron for loss of income, swearing that his luck had indeed turned. Subsequently, Elphin boasted to the King, Maelgwn, that his wife was the fairest woman in the kingdom, his horses the swiftest, and his poet the most wise. Maelgwn cast him into prison in silver chains, because he was noble. Taliesin vindicated Elphin and aided his release. Elphin's horse easily out-raced Maelgwn's steeds and, at the point where Elphin's jockey cast down his cap, Taliesin ordered men to dig. Below was discovered a cauldron of gold, richly compensating Elphin for his seemingly fruitless night at the weir. Elements of both Taliesin's and Elphin's story are embedded within the 'Preiddeu Annwn', which concerns the releasing of a youth in chains and an otherworld cauldron. [17, 80]

Elves (L) The Scandinavian form of fairy who were believed to be either of the helping or hindering variety. In Scottish folklore they appear as the *Seelie* (Blessed) or *Unseelie Court*. They lived in Elfame. J. R. R. Tolkien reintroduced the Elves in his fictional works, relating the Scandinavian name to the dwellers of the *Blessed Islands* in Celtic mythology. (See *Alfar*.) [44, 53]

Emer (I) Daughter of *Forgall*. She was wooed, in riddling dialogue, by *CuChulainn* when he was seven years old. Her father, Forgall, sent him to train with *Scathach* in order to be worthy of Emer. Although beloved of CuChulainn, she suffered much from his faithlessness with other women. Her 'only jealousy' was of his attachment to the otherworldy woman, *Fand*, who stole his affection. Both he and Emer were eventually given a draft by druids:

CuChulainn to forget Fand, and Emer to forget her jealousy. She upheld CuChulainn above all other heroes at *Bricriu*'s feast. Her lament at his death is one of the great ochones of Irish poetry. After delivering it she fell dead into his grave. [12, 160]

Endellion/Endelient (ST) (sixth century) Daughter of the legendary King Brychan. She was said to be the god-daughter of King *Arthur* who slew a man who had killed her cow, the milk of which was her only sustenance. She revived the malefactor. At her death she bade her friends lay her upon a cart whose resting place should be determined by the oxen which drew it: there she was buried. She is the patron of Saint Endellion in Cornwall and her feast-day is 29 April. [109]

Enid (A) Wife of *Gereint* in Chrétien de Troyes' Erec' and the Welsh 'Gereint ap Erbin'. He discovered her weeping because he preferred the luxury of home life rather than the rigours of knighthood, but Gereint believed her to be weeping for a lover. He took her with him on a series of adventures, forbidding her to speak to him, so that she was unable to warn of many dangers. They were finally reconciled. [17]

Eochaid Airem (I) King of Ireland. He took *Etain* from the *Sidhe* as his wife. *Midir*, her first husband, whom she had totally forgotten, came to play fidchell (chess) with Eochaid, letting him win many games and undertaking to perform servile work as the stake. He brought fairy oxen from the Sidhe to help clear the causeway which Eochaid demanded. Until that time, oxen had been yoked by a harness over their brows, but after seeing Midir's oxen, Eochaid proclaimed that all oxen should be yoked over their shoulders, thus earning himself the name Airem or Ploughman.

Lastly, Midir played a game of fidchell and demanded to hold Etain and a kiss as the winner's stake. Midir won but Etain refused to go with him without Eochaid relinquishing her of his own free will. He bade Midir kiss her in the hall in front of everyone. Midir seized Etain and flew with her out of the smoke-hole. Eochaid brought war against the Sidhe and eventually recovered Etain, but he earned the implacable hatred of the Sidhe which was vested upon succeeding generations of his kindred. [13, 99]

Eoghan Mor (I) He was nicknamed Mug Nuadat, or Slave (devotee) of *Nuadu*. He married *Beare*. He made a division of Ireland between himself and Conn, who had the northern portion, himself retaining 'the slave's half'.

Eostre (N) Anglo-Saxon goddess of Spring, worshipped at festivals all over Britain. She gave her name to Easter and some of the present folk-customs performed at that time may be traced to her cult.

Epona (C) Although her cult was more widespread in Europe, Epona, the goddess of horsemen and animals, found a special place in Britain — her mythos appearing in the stories of *Rhiannon* and *Macha*. She is depicted as a woman, semi-naked, seated on a horse, although sometimes she is seated on a throne, while two foals feed from her lap, echoing the frequent appearance of twins in stories connected with her. She was adopted by the Romans who observed her feast on 18 December. She was a favourite with cavalry regiments, especially those stationed in the Low Countries. Grooms decorated her shrines, to be found in every stable, with garlands of roses. One of her symbols is the key which unlocks the Underworld. [80]

Eremon (I) Son of *Miled*. He successfully fought his brother *Eber* for the kingship of Ireland. From him all later Irish kings descended. [15]

Eriu (I) Mother of *Bres*. She was associated with the royal seat of Uisnech in Meath. She was one of the three goddesses of *Sovereignty*, to whom *Amergin* promised the honour of naming the island. Her name is retained in the title of Ireland as Erin. [15]

Erthal (W) Chieftain of the 'Goddoddin', the great heroic epic of post-Arthurian Britain. He is described thus: 'In the van was, loud as thunder, the din of shields - when the tale shall be told of the battle of Catraeth (Catterick), the people will utter sighs, long has been their grief because of the warrior's absence, there will be a dominion without a sovereign and a smoking land.' [190]

Esras (I) The master of wisdom who gave into *Lugh*'s keeping the spear which gave victory in battle. He dwelt in *Gorias*, one of the four cities from which the *Tuatha de Danaan* had come. The Book of Invasions suggests that this was in the northern Isles of Greece.

Estmere (L) Hero of a late medieval Scottish romance. Something of an adventurer, he journeys to the court of King Asland to ask for his daughter's hand. This is refused but not before the two have fallen in love. Shortly afterwards, Estmere learns that a Spanish prince is threatening King Asland and his daughter, and disguising himself as a Moorish harper he infiltrates the castle, slays the Spaniard and wins the hand of the lady. Witty and lighthearted romance full of magic and colourful adventures. [196]

Etain (I) The wife of *Midir*, one of the *Sidhe*. She was enchanted by Midir's other wife, *Fuamnach*, into the shape of a fly which was tossed about the world, until it fell into the cup of the Etair's wife who drank it and later bore a daughter called Etain. She later became the wife of *Eochaid Airem*. Midir came and played fidchell (chess) with Eochaid in order to win her back. He eventually succeeded and they fled back to the sidhe in the form of *swans*. There are variant legends which tell of her different reincarnations, but she is always called Etain in each one. [13]

Etheldreda/Aethelthryth/Ediltrudis/Audrey (ST) (d.679) Abbess of Ely. This formidable daughter of King Anna of the East Angles became something of a professional virgin. She was married to Tond-berht, and elderman, who died leaving her virgin. She was then married to King Egfrith of Northumbria who had agreed to her remaining a virgin but after twelve years requested that she sleep with him. She then founded the double monastery of Ely, leaving her husband. Fairs held in her honour led to the expression 'tawdry' after the cheap fairings sold there. She is depicted with two does who were said to have sustained the Ely community with their milk during a famine. Her feast-day is 23 June.

Ethniu (I) Ethniu's curious legend is clearly overlaid by later Christian influence. It tells that she was brought to Brugh na Boinne to be the foster-sister of *Manannan mac Lir*'s daughter. She took no nourishment of any kind and it was discovered that a De Danaan chief had tried to rape her, thus awaking a pure nature within her. She existed solely as a spirit. *Angus Og* and Manannan went on a quest, returning with two magical cows whose milk never dried up and she lived on this. She left the Brugh one day and found herself unable to enter it again. She thereafter became a Christian and met Saint *Patrick* who administered extreme unction to her. She is ever aware of her former people calling and seeking for her. [182]

Excalibur (A) *Arthur*'s magical sword, received from the *Lady of the Lake*. As long as he carried it no one could defeat him but the scabbard, which preserved its bearer from wounds, was stolen by *Morgan le Fay*. Its name means 'cut-steel'. It is also called *Caliburnus* or *Caledfwlch*. It is often confused with the Sword in the Stone by which Arthur was inaugurated as King. That sword broke in battle necessitating that Arthur find another. It was sometimes said to have been made by *Wayland*. [84]

F

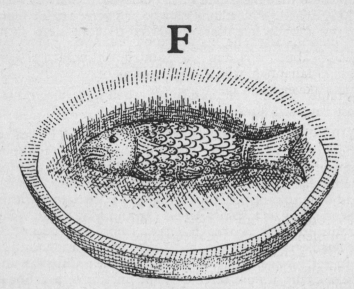

Fisher King's Dish

Faery (L) The dwelling place of the *Fairies*, considered to be the inner realm bordering on earthly domains, into which human beings sometimes stray. (See Robert *Kirk*). The rules for entering Faery relate to almost all other realms of otherworldly beings: the entrant must take an implement of iron, usually a knife; he must not partake of food or drink; he must behave courteously among its inhabitants. If he observes these rules he can emerge into his own place again. [44, 55, 71, 81]

Fafnir (N) Son of the Dwarf King, Hreidmar. *Loki* killed his brother Otr and had to cover him with gold in recompense. This caused dissension between Fafnir and another brother, Regin. Fafnir turned himself into a dragon in order to keep the gold. He was later slain by the hero Sigurd. [7]

Fairies (L) This word derives from 'Fays' meaning the Fatae or Fates. Although latterly fairies have been understood as diminutive beings inhabiting flowers etc., their true stature, both actual and mythical, is considerably greater. They are the British version of the Irish *Sidhe* dwellers, bestowing gifts of prophecy and music, living in bliss in their own fairy hills. According to oral tradition, they originate from the angels of the Fall or are children of Adam by Lilith, the elder brethren of humanity who are neither divine nor human, but none the less immortal. [44, 55, 71, 81]

Falias (I) It was one of four cities from whence the *Tuatha de Danaan* came to Ireland. Its master of wisdom was called *Morfessa*, and it was from here that the Stone of Fal derived. (See *Hallows*.) [5]

Fand (I) The sister of *Labraid* and wife of *Manannan*. She was given to *CuChulainn* after he had helped *Labraid*. *Emer* taunted CuChulainn about this new love and he relinquished her. She returned to Manannan, who shook his cloak between the lovers that they might never again meet. [12, 99]

Fedelm (I) She was the witch who had the fostering of *Corc*. It was while he was in her care that he gained his name for one night, when her sister witches were assembling, one of them called out 'I bless everything, except what is under the *cauldron*.' Corc was singed by the blast of the fire on one ear, thus earning the name 'Red'.

Fenris (N) The monstrous offspring of *Loki* and the giantess *Angrboda*. He took the form of a giant wolf, who is said to appear at the last moment of *Ragnarok* to consume the world of the gods. He was bound by a chain, made by the dwarfs have been, from the roots of a mountain, the sound of a cat mewing and a fish's breath. It was as thin as silk but as strong as creation itself. The god *Tyr*, who bound him, lost a hand in the process. [7, 53]

Fercetrniu (I) He was the poet of *Cu Roi*. When he discovered that *Blanaid* had been responsible for his master's death, he seized her and together they plunged off the cliffs of the Beare Peninsula to their deaths.

Ferdiad (I) The oldest friend and companion-in-arms of *CuChulainn*, with whom he was taught at the court of *Scathach* in Alba. He was of Connacht and found himself forced to combat CuChulainn at the ford, when Ulster was being attacked by *Maeve* for the possession of the Brown *Bull* of Daire. They fought for three days; at the end of each day they bathed each other's wounds and slept in the same blanket. But at the last CuChulainn used his great spear, the Gae Bolg, against which no man could stand. CuChulainn had asked his charioteer, *Loegaire*, to incite his anger with insults and gibes and it was so that Ferdiad died at his friend's hand. [12, 27]

Fergus mac Roigh (I) King of Ulster before *Nessa* begged him to relinquish his reign for one year, in favour of her son *Conchobar* who thereafter ruled and Fergus was permanently dethroned. For this insult, Fergus helped *Maeve* and the forces of Connacht. Because he was one of *CuChulainn*'s fosterers and teachers, he refused to engage in combat with him at the ford, making an agreement to spare CuChulainn if CuChulainn agreed to let him run away on a later occasion. He was the messenger of Conchobar to persuade *Deirdriu* and the sons of *Usnach* to return to Ulster. He was slain at the instigation of *Ailill* who found him swimming with Maeve in a lake. [5, 6]

Ferrishyn (C) The Manx name for the *Fairy* host. Their hearing was omniscient and for this reason, people would speak very carefully or quietly about them.

Fferyllt (W) Often translated as the *Fairies*, Fferyllt is probably derived from the Welsh for Virgil 'Fferyll', who had a reputation in medieval times for being a magician and alchemist. *Ceridwen* is said to have consulted the books of the Fferyllt in preparing her *cauldron* of inspiration which *Gwion* drank. 'Fferyllt' means chemist in modern Welsh. [55, 80]

Fflur (W) Nearly all traces of Fflur's legend have been lost. Her name, meaning Flower, establishes her as one with the other Flower Maidens of British mythology — *Blanaid, Guinevere, Blodeuwedd*. She was beloved of *Caswallawn*, but was carried off by Julius Caesar, according to the meagre evidence of the 'Triads'. Caswallawn's quest in search of her, even to the gates of Rome, suggests that Fflur may indeed be one of the many faces of *Sovereignty*. [28, 80]

Fiachna (I) Son of *Lir* and *Aobh*. He was turned into a *swan* by his step-mother, *Aoife*.

Fianna/Fenians (I) The warband of Ireland, composed of 150 chiefs, each having under them twenty-seven men. The requirements for joining the Fianna were vigorous. Each man had to know by heart the poet's repertoire, submit to an initiatory test of his skills and courage, including having spears thrown at him, and being able to withdraw a thorn from his foot while stooping under a low branch and running. Besides warriors, they had druids, physicians and musicians amongst their number. As it was a warband which upheld the country, each man was free of tribal retribution if he killed a member of any family, nor might his own family avenge him if he was killed on active service. The most famous leader of the *Fianna* was *Fionn mac Cumhal* — they are analogous to the *Round Table Knights* and King *Arthur*. [8, 13, 21]

Findabair (I) Daughter of *Ailill* and *Maeve*. She loved *Fraoch* but he would not pay her dowry, until bribed by Maeve, he agreed to take her in return for his help in battle against Ulster. Secretly Maeve offered Findabair to every champion who would fulfil this task, but all refused, save Fraoch, because they knew they would face the invincible *CuChulainn*. When that hero killed Fraoch, Findabair died of a broken heart. [27]

Findias (I) It was one of the four cities from which the *Tuatha de Danaan* came to Ireland. Its master of wisdom, *Uscias*, gave *Nuadu* his sword. (See *Hallows*.) [5]

Fingal (S) *Fionn mac Cumhal* is sometimes called this in Gaelic Scotland. The name also derived some popularity from the bogus epic, 'Ossian', written by MacPherson in the late eighteenth century; drawing on oral stories about the *Fianna*. James MacPherson fabricated a set of romantic Celtic poems which impressed and fired Europe to a reconsideration of Celtic culture, though his work was soon discovered to be a fake.

Finneces/Finegas (I) A poet who lived by the Boyne. He guarded the *salmon* of knowledge for seven years, knowing that whoever ate of it would have all knowledge. His pupil, *Demne (Fionn mac Cumhal* in disguise) helped him roast it and sucked his thumb where the hot juices spurted out upon him. And so Fionn gained all knowledge. [13, 104]

Finnbhenach (I) The arch-enemy of *Donn Cuailgne*. Finnbhenach had been through many incarnations, in many shapes, before he became a white *bull*. Together they were the cause of strife between *Maeve* and *Ailill*.

Fintan (I) Survivor of the Flood, father of *Cessair*. He hid in a cave in the form of a *salmon*. He passed through countless transformations, remembering all that had passed in Ireland. He appeared to later Irishmen who were disputing the ordering of Ireland and told them her entire history and the associations each place had had. [15, 99]

Fionn mac Cumhal/Finn mac Cool (I) Son of Cumhal and *Muirne*. He was fostered by a druidess, Bodhmall, and a woman-warrior, Liath Luachra, who taught him battle-skills and the Arts. Calling himself *Demne*, he went to learn poetry of *Finneces* and obtained the thumb of knowledge; acquired by sucking his thumb when the *salmon* of knowledge was roasting for Finneces to consume. In following years, he had only to chew his thumb to have foreknowledge of events. His two hounds, Bran and Sceolan, were really his nephews in dog-form, because they had human knowledge they were wiser than all other dogs. He became head of the *Fianna*, fighting all the enemies of Ireland.

He was father of *Oisin* by *Sadbh*. His attempt to marry *Grainne* failed because he was ageing and she eloped with *Diarmuid*. He pursued them both and brought about Diarmuid's death. He outlived his grandson *Oscar* and saw the slaughter of his Fianna at the Battle of Gabhra. He did not die but wasted away into the Otherworld

where, like *Arthur*, he is said to sleep. He is credited with building
the causeway between Ireland and Scotland, where he appears in
many local folk-stories as the ever-living and cunning hero. *Mongan*
is said to be a later reincarnation of Fionn. His many adventures
cannot be detailed here. [8, 13, 21, 104, 159]

Fionnuala (I) Daughter of *Lir* and *Aobh*. She was turned into a *swan*,
along with her brothers, *Aed, Conn* and *Fiachra*, by *Aoife*, her step-
mother, destined to roam the world for 900 years. Together they
flew across the waters with no place to shelter, lamenting the joys
of the *Sidhe*. At last they heard the bell of *Mochaomhog*'s church
pealing. He caused silver chains to be made for their necks, and so
accoutred, they used to attend mass. At last all the conditions set
by Aoife for their term of enchantment were met. A man from the
North and a woman from the South came together and wished to
possess the swans. The man, Lairgren, angered at Mochaomhog's
refusal to relinquish them from his care, laid hands on two.
Immediately the swans became 900-year-old men and women,
withered beyond belief. Mochaomhog baptized them immediately
and buried them. [13]

Fir Chlis (S) The Nimble Men or Merry Dancers were the names
given by Highlanders to the Aurora Borealis. They were considered
to be the souls of fallen angels whose descent had been arrested
before they reached the earthly realms, though their glory was considered due to the blood spilt between their rival clans. [44]

Fir Dhearg (I) The Red Men are the prototypes of the now devalued
leprachaun. Dressed in red, they were nearly always at pains to trick
mortals and play tricks upon them, but they could sometimes be
compelled to lend assistance.

Firbolg (I) Literally 'the people of the bag'. They settled in Ireland,
fleeing Greece where they had been enslaved and made to carry earth
in bags. They afterwards made ships out of these bags and sailed
to Spain. They held Ireland after the death of *Nemed* until the
coming of the *Tuatha de Danaan*. [15]

Fisher King (A) The name given to the *Grail King* after he fed a
multitude of followers from a single fish. The name may have arisen
from a play on the French terms 'pêcheur' (fisherman) and 'pêcheur'
(sinner), since the *Wasteland* is caused by the king's sin or blemish.
(See *Wounded King*.) [82, 83]

Flaitheas (I) This name is what the Goddess of *Sovereignty* calls
herself when she meets *Niall*. It means 'lordship' or 'sovereignty'.
Frequently, in Irish tradition, candidate kings are offered a cup to
drink from which is called the dergflaith or 'cup of red lordship',
which denotes their acceptability to the goddess. [186]

Florence (A) One of *Gawain*'s various illegitimate sons. In this instance, one of two such sons by the unnamed sister of a *Round Table Knight* called Brandiles. He is supposed to have joined the attempt to entrap *Lancelot* in the Queen's chamber, and was killed by Lancelot during his escape.

Foawr (C) The Manx form of the *Fomorians*. They were considered to be a race of stone-throwing giants.

Fodla (I) One of the three goddesses of *Sovereignty* to whom *Amergin* promised the honour of naming Ireland. (See *Banba* and *Eriu*.)

Fomorians (I) The original inhabitants of Ireland who lived beyond the sea or under it, according to legend. Various of the invading peoples were attacked by them, particularly the *Tuatha de Danaan* with whom they came to pitch battle. Their king was *Balor*. They were probably a remembrance of the earliest native peoples, of non-Celtic stock; they accumulated every possible association with evil and darkness in legend. [13]

Forgall (I) Father of *Emer*. He sent *CuChulainn* to learn arms of *Scathach*, confident that he would not return alive. But the hero returned, killed Forgall and married Emer. [12]

Fortunate Islands (C) Like the *Blessed Islands:* the earthly paradise located variously to the west of Ireland or applied to the Canary or Madeira Islands. According to the 'Vita Merlini', it is ruled over by *Morgan* and her nine attendant muses. Analogous to *Avalon*. [29, 111]

Fraoch (I) He was loved by *Findabair*, daughter of *Ailill* and *Maeve*. He refused to pay a bride-price for her but agreed to accept her if he helped Maeve beat the Ulstermen. He was killed by *CuChulainn*. [27]

Frey (N) God of fertility, sunshine and growth; patron of married couples. He was the son of *Njord*, the sea-god, and *Nerthus*, and the twin brother of *Freya*. He lived in *Alfhelm* and ruled over the *Lios Alfar*. He was given a golden *boar*, Gullian-bursti, by the dwarves. He also possessed a magic ship, Skidbladnir, which travelled anywhere in the world and could contain all the gods, although it could also be folded up into a pocket when not in use. [53]

Freya (N) Goddess of love and fecundity, daughter of *Njord* and *Nerthus*; twin sister of *Frey*. She married Odur (Sunshine) and had two daughters, Hnoss and Gersemi. It is said that she wept tears of amber and gold when her husband left her. She could also fly taking the shape of a falcon at will. She lived in a house named Sessyrymnir, in the realm of Folkvang. [53]

Friar Bacon (L) An historical figure who became the subject of a romance in which he was accredited with various magical activities and abilities, including the creation of a Bronze Head which uttered prophecies. The suggestion that this was initially to help protect England suggests a memory of the Celtic god *Bran*, whose head was buried under White Mount at the Tower of London to protect the land. Bacon, who was in reality a scholar and alchemist, lived in the thirteenth century. He finally retired to a life of seclusion.

Frigga (N) Goddess of clouds, sky, married love and housewives. According to some versions she was the daughter of *Njord* and *Odin*, although she later became Odin's wife. They had four children: *Hermod*, *Baldur*, *Hodur* and *Tyr*. Variant texts say that they had seven children who founded seven Saxon kingdoms in England; thus Frigga is considered of particular importance to British mythology. She had particular care for humanity and through her eleven hand-maids kept watch over their lives. In her house, Fensalir, she spun golden thread and rainbow clouds. [53]

Frost Giants (N) Perpetual enemies of the *Aesir*. The origin of their enmity seems lost in the ages before the creation of humanity. It was believed that at the end of time, they would invade *Asgard* and that in the ensuing battle both gods and giants would perish. This event was known as *Ragnarok*. They are the Norse Titans, concerned with both the beginning and ending of the world.

Fuamnach (I) Wife of *Midir* of the *Sidhe*. She was jealous of *Etain*, Midir's other wife and enchanted her into the shape of a fly. Midir beheaded Fuamnach when he discovered her treachery. [13]

Fuath (S) These malicious spirits were found near water, both inland and sea-water. Fuaths were thought to be the parents of *Brollachans*.

Fulk Fitzwarin (L) Actual historical character who lived at the time of King John Lackland and was one of the barons who opposed his greedy rule. He later became the subject of a lengthy romance in which his adventures with *dragons* and witches, monsters and beautiful maidens dressed his life with a border of myth and legend. He has many parallels with Robin Hood and seems for a time to have lived the life of a real outlaw. He is one of the few characters who really deserve the description Norman rather than English or Saxon.

G

Glastonbury and the Grail

Gabriel Hounds/Ratchets (L) The hounds of the *Wild Hunt* which are heard yelping in the sky, sometimes believed to be the cries of migrating geese. These hounds are like those hunted by *Arawn*, King of *Annwn*, having red-tipped ears. (See *Gwynn ap Nudd*.)

Gaheris of Orkney (A) The third son of *Morgause* and *Lot* of Orkney: brother of *Gawain*, *Agravaine* and *Gareth*. He was accidentally slain by *Lancelot* during the rescue of *Guinevere* from the stake. [20]

Galahad (A) One of the three successful *Grail Knights*. He was the son of *Lancelot* and *Elaine of Corbenic*. Although he was born out of wedlock, he was a pure knight who was never defeated in battle. He surpassed the deeds of his father, who was unworthy to see the *Grail* because of his adultery with *Guinevere*, and he can be seen as an extension of Lancelot into the spiritual worlds. He died when he had seen the Grail and was buried in *Sarras*. [20, 24, 83]

Galahaut, the Haute Prince (A) He was *Arthur*'s enemy but after his defeat at the hands of *Lancelot*, he became a devoted follower of that knight. He arranged the first secret meeting of the lovers and eventually died of grief when he heard a false report of Lancelot's death. [20, 23]

Galehodin (A) Only brother to *Lancelot*. He had a rather undistinguished career but was presented with the dukedom of Saintongue by Lancelot himself, who assumed the role of ruler over that country during his later days.

Gamelyn (L) A famous medieval outlaw whose adventures rivalled those of the better known *Robin Hood*. Youngest son of a baron, Gamelyn is disinherited by a grasping older brother and is thereafter at war with all his siblings save one, Sir Ote, who befriends him. But Gamelyn is a man of great strength and short temper and was soon in trouble with the law. At the instigation of one of his brothers he is thrown into prison, escapes and is declared an outlaw. Soon made King of the Outlaws, he lives a life of adventure until he finally wins justice for himself and Ote, regaining his lands but retaining a friendly relationship with the old outlaw band which he had once led.

Gan-Ceann (I) Gan-Ceann (without a head) is called the Love-Talker in some parts of Ireland. He appears in lovely places to single women and courts them, before leaving them as swiftly as he came, to pine away. [44]

Ganieda (A) *Merlin*'s sister in the 'Vita Merlini' who lived with him in the forest and prophesied coming events. Sometimes called Gwenddydd. [29, 111]

Gareth of Orkney (A) The fourth son of *Morgause* and *Lot* of Orkney. He came to *Arthur*'s court incognito and was named *Beaumains* (Fair Hands) by Sir *Kay*. He later proved himself a worthy hero and was knighted by *Lancelot* who, however, later slew him accidentally during the rescue of *Guinevere* from the stake. [20]

Gawain of Orkney (A) The eldest son of *Morgause* and *Lot* of Orkney. He was *Arthur*'s nephew and heir. In later medieval texts he became a blusterer and womanizer, but in earlier sources he was the Knight of the Goddess. His strength, like that of *CuChulainn*, with whom he has much in common, was said to grow greater towards the middle of the day, from which he has been classified as a 'sun hero'. In Welsh he is called *Gwalchmai* (Hawk of May). He was one of the earliest figures associated with Arthur. Two of his greatest adventures are his combat with the *Green Knight*, and his encounter and marriage with Dame *Ragnell*. [14, 17, 20, 25, 76]

Gefjon/Gefion (N) Goddess of agriculture who also presided over virgins who were gathered to her hall after their deaths. She was attendant to *Frigga* and had four sons by a giant. When on a certain occasion she asked a king for some land, he promised her all she could plough in a day. She turned her sons into oxen and ploughed a great tract of land which was then towed out to sea.

It forms the present island of Seeland. Gefjon later married one of *Odin*'s sons and founded a royal line of Denmark. [53]

Gelorwydd (W) A warrior in the 'Goddoddin', the great Celtic epic of battle and bravery. He is called 'the Gem of Baptism' because he gave extreme unction to the dying on the field of battle with his own blood. [190]

Genius Cucullatus/Genii Cucullati (RB) This figure or triplicity of figures is unnamed, but they appear as attendant upon a Mother Goddess in Romano-British reliefs, sometimes offering her eggs. They are always dressed in short, hooded cloaks. They may have associations with pace-egging rituals, but their function is probably that of healing, and of heralds to the Underworld. [60, 103, 119]

George (ST) (third/fourth century) Patron of England. He was martyred at Lydda in Palestine by being shod in red-hot shoes, broken on a spiked wheel and immersed in quick-lime. The legend of his having slain a *dragon* was very popular: he rescued a king's daughter from becoming the dragon's tribute and so managed to convert her people. Richard I (the Lionheart) was said to have had a vision of him and was able to restore the saint's tomb at Lydda. Edward III inaugurated the Order of the Garter under his patronage, and in 1415, Saint George was proclaimed chief patron of England when English soldiers, under Henry V, won the battle of Agincourt. Many mumming plays portray him in their dramatis personae as the hero-king who fights for England, overcoming the invading Saracen. His feast-day is 23 April.

Gereint (W) Son of Erbin. He is the hero of the story 'Gereint and Enid', which Chrétien de Troyes also treated in 'Erec and Enide'. He championed a maiden whose father had been deprived of his living, and brought her to court. *Arthur* and his men had been out hunting the White Hart, and it was decided that its head should be presented to the fairest maiden: Gwenhwyfar gave it to *Enid* who married Gereint. Gereint then took her for his wife and they retired to his estates.

Misunderstanding Enid's regret at his retiring from an active life, Gereint assumed she had a lover and wished to be rid of him. He immediately set out on a journey, taking her with him and bidding her to be silent. Throughout many adventures and dangers, during which he refused to listen to her warnings, Gereint continued to mistreat her. Finally they came to Earl *Owain*'s castle where enchanted games were held within a hedge of mist.

Despite Owain's caution that none had ever returned thence, Gereint entered the magic hedge which was ringed with heads on stakes. There he found an orchard where a maiden sat in a golden chair. Gereint seated himself beside her and was challenged by a knight. He beat the knight and blew a horn which hung in the orchard, causing the games to cease forever. He was reconciled with Enid. Gereint was said to have died in battle at Llongborth (Langport, Somerset), possibly supporting Arthur against the Saxons. [17, 33, 80]

Gilfaethwy (W) Son of *Don*. He desired his uncle *Math*'s footholder, *Goewin*. His brother, *Gwydion*, helped him obtain her by raising war between Gwynedd and Dyfed. For his punishment, Gilfaethwy was changed, successively, into a hind, a *boar*, and a wolf-bitch and bore young to Gwydion who had been similarly enchanted. [17, 80]

Ginnungagap (N) A fathomless chasm between *Niflheim* and *Muspellsheim*. Cold winds rising from this dreadful place turned to blocks of ice which could be heard as thunder when they ground against each other. In Muspellsheim, the flame giant *Surtr*, striking sparks from his sword, made steam rise from the ice. This in turn became hoar-frost and began to fill the chasm. It was said that the gods gave life to this material, which became the *Frost Giant, Ymir*, and when he came to die, his body and blood became the earth and sea. [53]

Giolla Deacair (I) He was an otherworld champion whose *horse* was unridable. Only *Conan* was able to mount it, with the intention of riding it to death. It carried him to *Tir Tairngire* where *Fionn* had to come and rescue him. [13, 21]

Glaistyn (C) A Manx form of the *each-uisge*. The Glaistyn had the ability to appear in human form which, though fair and handsome, was betrayed by the horse-like ears. (See *Kelpie*.) [44]

Glastonbury (A) The town in Somerset which is traditionally associated with *Arthur* and the Holy *Grail*. Many stories are told of its magical properties and it has become something of a pilgrimage spot in recent years. Its name probably derives from Ynys Witrin (Isle of Glass) and it has been identified by some authorities with *Avalon. Joseph of Arimathea* is believed to have brought the chalice, used by Christ to celebrate the Last Supper, to Glastonbury which became the first shrine of the Grail. In 1191 some bones, believed to be those of *Arthur* and *Guinevere*, were exhibited by the monks. A plaque still marks the spot today but such a discovery is anathema to tradition for the British expect Arthur's return: 'unknown, unwise, a grave for Arthur', says an old Welsh poem, 'The Stanzas on the Graves'. [33, 34, 82]

Glewlwyd Gafaelfawr (W) *Arthur*'s gatekeeper or porter 'at the calends of January' — a task which he shared with four other men, according to 'Culhwch and Olwen', wherein he has a riddling dialogue with *Culhwch*. There is a direct parallel between this exchange and that which *Lugh* is submitted to when he seeks to gain entrance to the hall of *Nuadu*. [17, 80, 84]

Gobhan Saor (I) Analogous to *Goibniu* and *Gofannon*. He lives on as Gobhan Saor, a crafty smith or mason whose skill outwits the unwary. He is a favourite character in Irish folk-stories. [149]

Gobhnet (ST) (fifth century) She was a nun who was instructed that she should build her oratory where she found nine white *deer* grazing. This place was Ballyvourney where she also kept her bee-hives: the bees acted as her watchdogs and drove thieves away. Her holy well is still visited and her feast-day is 11 February.

Godiva, Lady (F) Godgifu, wife of Leofric of Mercia. Her husband tyrannized the church and extracted heavy taxes from the people of Coventry. Godgifu begged him to relent and he agreed to do so if she would ride naked through Coventry on market-day. Clothed only in her hair, she did so and the citizens of Coventry averted their eyes, all except Peeping Tom who was stricken blind. [98, 120]

Goewin (W) The virgin footholder of *Math* who was raped by *Gilfaethwy*. In order to compensate her for her disgrace, Math married her. [17, 80]

Gofannon (W) Son of *Don*. His story has become displaced from all but the meagre information of the 'Triads' wherein he is described as the accidental slayer of his nephew, *Dylan*. Gofannon is the Welsh eqivalent of *Goibniu*, and was a god of smithcraft. [17, 80]

Gogmagog (L) A giant who broke in upon the festivities of the newly landed *Brutus* and attacked his company. *Corineus* wrestled with him and cast him into the sea. Gog and Magog were the names of two effigies kept at London Guildhall since the reign of Henry V. These were destroyed in the Great Fire and were replaced by smaller effigies in 1708. [9]

Goibniu (I) The smith of the *Tuatha de Danaan*. He forged the weapons by which the *Fomorians* were overcome. He killed *Ruadan*, the son of *Brigit* and of *Bres*, who had been sent to spy on his armoury and to kill him. Goibniu was healed of his wounds in the well of Slane. He is analogous to Welsh *Gofannon*. [5, 99]

Goleuddydd (W) Mother of *Culhwch*. She gave birth to him after running mad in the forest and being frightened by *pigs*. Her mythos bears a marked resemblance to the mother of *Tristan*. [17, 80]

Goll mac Morna (I) Slayer of Cumhal, *Fionn*'s father and head of the *Fianna*. He lost one of his eyes at Cumhal's hand. He later willingly relinquished his position in favour of Fionn whom he befriended without rancour. But at the last the feud between the two men caused the ending of the Fianna. [13, 21]

Goon Desert (A) According to the 'Conte del Graal' of Chrétien de Troyes, Goon Desert was the father of the *Grail* maiden and the brother of the *Fisher King*. However, his behaviour hardly matches up to that of a Grail guardian as he was responsible for the murder of a knight named Espinogee, whose nephew later took revenge upon him. When his body was brought home his daughter prophesied that the sword which had slain him, which was broken, would only be mended when the Grail was achieved. Her uncle, hastily picking up the pieces of broken blade, is wounded in the thigh by them. His wound, along with the sword, is only mended when *Perceval* comes to the castle of Quiguagrant, which had been Goon Desert's home. [4]

Goreu (W) Son of *Custennin* and an unnamed woman who was sister to *Igraine*. Goreu was one of twenty-four sons, all of whom were killed by *Yspaddaden Pencawr*, he alone escaping because his mother hid him in a cupboard. In 'Culhwch and Olwen' is he unnamed at the outset. He goes as a champion to Cei (cf. *Kay*) who promises to guard the boy. During the fulfilment of one of Culhwch's tasks, the boy achieves a great feat of fighting through three courtyards of men to reach his companions who acclaim him 'The Best' or Goreu. This feat may once have been associated with the winning of the Sword or Glaive of Light, one of the *Hallows*. Goreu finally beheads Yspaddaden, avenging his father, Custennin. [17, 80]

Gorias (I) One of the cities from which the *Tuatha De Danaan* came before coming to Ireland. Its master of wisdom was *Esras*, who provided the spear of *Lugh*. (See *Hallows*.) [5]

Gorlois of Cornwall (A) Duke of Cornwall and husband of *Igerna* on whom *Uther Pendragon* doted. With the help of *Merlin*, Uther was disguised in Gorlois' likeness and lay with Igerna. Her child was *Arthur*. Gorlois was slain at the moment of the child's conception. He was father of *Morgan, Morgause* and *Elaine of Garlot*. [20]

Gowther (A) Hero of a little known Arthurian romance in which he is the son of a fiendish knight and a gently born lady. The boy proves to be of a savage disposition until the devilish tendencies are driven out of him by means of a self-inflicted penance. A rather pious story, but an interesting reflection of the way in which the chivalric romances were used as teaching aids by the Church. [190]

Grail (A) One of the *Hallows* of Britain. It has become an almost univeral symbol of spiritual search and aspiration. Believed to derive from earlier, pagan, *cauldrons*, it became identified with the cup used by Christ to celebrate the Last Supper and First Eucharist, and which later caught his blood at the deposition from the Cross. Its guardian was *Joseph of Arimathea*, who is believed to have brought it to Britain and there made a shrine for it at *Glastonbury*. It was later sought by the *Grail Knights* of the *Round Table*. It is still sought as an inner reality by people today.

The Grail manifested itself only to those worthy of it, when the country had fallen into a *wasteland*. During times of prosperity and good government, it was guarded by the *Grail Kings* or guardians, and was said to be 'withdrawn'. Its appearance is dependent on the state of kingship (*Wounded King*) and the gifts of *Sovereignty*. [24, 26, 82, 83]

Grail King (A) The *Grail*'s manifestation in and relationship to the earthly realms is dependent upon its guardian, or Grail King. This function was fulfilled by a line of Grail guardians, drawn from one family — usually that of *Joseph of Arimathea*. It succeeds to *Arthur*'s knights who are successful *Grail Knights*, *Perceval* and *Galahad*. It follows that those who find the Grail become its guardians. The early Grail Kings include *Bran the Blessed*, *Pellam*, *Anfortas* and *Brons*. In Welsh tradition, this role is assigned to *Manawyddan* and *Pryderi*. Each guardian or king is wounded: his mortality sits heavy upon him since he has tasted immortal things. When he passes on the role to his successor, he himself passes within to the Blessed Realms. [81, 83]

Grail Knights/Questers (A) In the later *Grail* cycles *Galahad* is the Grail-winner, with *Perceval* and *Bors* as his companions, but in the earlier tales it is Perceval who is the sole successful Grail-winner. There were many other unsuccessful knights on the quest, including *Gawain* and *Lancelot*. [24, 83]

Grail Lance (A) The weapon with which the Roman centurion, Longinus, pierced the side of Christ on the Cross. It subsequently became one of the *Hallows* of the *Grail*, and was sought together with that object in *Arthur*'s time. Fragments of a spear, said to be that of Longinus, were housed in the Vatican museum. The lance is related, natively, to the shining spear of *Lugh* or *Llew*, which came from *Findias* with the *Tuatha de Danaan*. [82, 83]

Grail Question (A) The *Wasteland* and the *Wounded King* can only be healed when someone asks the Grail question. Usually the Grail-seeker is seated at a banquet when the *Hallows* of the Grail are processed to the accompaniment of much mourning. The unworthy candidate usually remains silent, but the successful one is supposed to ask 'what does this mean?' This question is a perennial one since it should be applied to all material and spiritual problems, in order that they be solved and come to terms with. Both *Perceval* and *Galahad* successfully discovered the answer.

Grail Sword (A) One of the *Grail Hallows*, sought by the Knights of the *Round Table* in their quest for the Grail. It was eventually found by *Gawain*, broken in two pieces; his quest subsequently was to mend the sword, which he did by taking it to its place of origin, the forge of *Wayland*. *Perceval* had a similar quest to mend the sword. It is natively associated with the Sword of Light, or the sword of *Nuadu*, the original Celtic *Wounded King*. [83]

Grainne (I) Daughter of *Cormac mac Art*. She was promised in marriage to *Fionn mac Cumhal*, but when she saw his greying hair she wondered whether it was more fitting for her to marry his son, *Oisin*. She saw *Diarmuid* in the wedding party and, having given the company a sleeping draught, she laid a geasa upon him to run away with her. Their long flight from Fionn was aided by *Angus mac Og*, Diarmuid's foster-father. There are numerous cairns and stone-circles in Ireland which bear the name 'the Bed of Diarmuid and Grainne', attesting to the prohibition set on them by Fionn, that they might not sleep in the same place on two consecutive nights. [13, 159]

Granuaile (1530–1603) Grace O'Malley was heir to the great seafaring clan of the O'Malleys of Clare. She forsook the role of wife and mother — although she was both — to sail her own fleet of ships which kept up a long harassing of Elizabethan overlords of Ireland. Her defence of Irish customs and rights saw her many times imprisoned for piracy. Her great popularity with the people immortalized her in song and story. She was supposed to keep her ship tied up by a clew to her big toe. Legend also credits her with meeting Elizabeth I to whom she was presented at Greenwich and with whom she shared many forthright characteristics. Elizabeth granted her a charter which gave Grace *carte blanche* to sail the Western Seas, to the dismay of Elizabeth's own commander, Sir Richard Bingham who had unsuccessfully fought Granuaile for years. [50]

Green Children The chronicler, Roger of Coggeshall tells of how a boy and a girl with green skin were found near a pit in Saint Mary of the Wolf-Pit. They would eat nothing but green food and spoke a foreign language. The boy died quite soon but the girl learned to talk and eat ordinary food, so that she became as an ordinary person and spoke of a land very like that described by *Elidor* in his adventures in *Faery*. [32, 44]

Green Knight (A) The fearsome, green-clad, green-skinned figure who came to *Arthur*'s court and offered to play the *Beheading Game* — an exchange of blows in which the challenger offered to have his head cut off in return for a similar beheading of the opponent. Only *Gawain* accepted the challenge. He was allowed a year's grace before being given the return blow.

Finding refuge at a castle, he was royally entertained by Lady

Bertilak who offered him a protective baldric before meeting the Green Knight. Gawain did not know that the Green Knight was really his host, Sir *Bertilak*. Gawain won the game but, because he had shamefully accepted Lady Bertilak's help, had to wear on his arms for ever, the Green Baldric or Green Garter (the endless knot or five-pointed star). The Green Knight revealed his true identity and that he had been enchanted by *Morgan le Fay*. This story stems directly from that of *CuChulainn*'s challenge to *Cu Roi mac Daire* at *Bricriu*'s feast. *Gromer Somer Joure* and *Hafgan* are analogous figures. [14, 25]

Grendel (N) Water-monster against which *Beowulf* struggled at the behest of the Danish king Hrothgar. Grendel lived beneath the North Sea with his mother, an even more terrible creature, whom Beowulf also successfully fought. [162]

Griflet (A) One of the first knights to be made by *Arthur* after his crowning, though the King seemed reluctant to do so because of Griflet's youth (he was the same age as Arthur). *Merlin* also commended him, and when an adventure occurred which Griflet wished to try his strength upon, warned Arthur that he may not return from it. He did survive and was the subject of a long romance (where he is called *Jaufre*) in which he wins and marries 'The Fair Brunnisend'. [20]

Grisandole (A) See *Avenable*.

Gromer Somer Joure (A) Powerful, magical shape-shifter who captured *Arthur* in the story of 'Gawain and Dame Ragnell'. He demanded that Arthur discovered what it was that women most desired. Arthur was told by the *Loathly Lady*, *Ragnell*, who demanded marriage with *Gawain* as her reward. Gromer's name means 'Lord of the Summer's Day'. He is analogous to *Hafgan* in the story of *Pwyll*, and bears many similarities with Gawain's other adversary, the *Green Knight*. Gromer was under enchantment by *Morgan*. [14, 80]

Gronw Pebr (W) The lover of *Blodeuwedd* and slayer of *Llew*. When Llew was resuscitated by *Gwydion*, be begged mercy and was allowed to hold a large stone between himself and Llew's spear, but the weapon passed through both stone and man. [17, 80]

Gruagach (S) 'The Hairy One'. The Gruagach appears in Scottish folklore as a kind of *brownie* or sometimes as a clever, green- or red-dressed man. He appears to be an otherworldly being of great magical power, able to enchant the unwary but also to aid mortals. He sometimes appears as the challenger and teacher of the boy-hero of folk-story, whom he provokes and is eventually outwitted by. Occasionally he appears as a giant. [44, 78]

Guendolena (L) Daughter of *Corineus*. She was deserted by her husband, *Locrinus*, in favour of his mistress, Estrildis. Guendolena drowned her and killed Locrinus in battle. She ruled briefly before giving her realm to the hands of her son. [9]

Guendolena/Gwendolena (A) *Merlin*'s wife. She married *Rhydderch Hael* after Merlin ran mad. [111]

Guinevere (A) Daughter of *Leodegrance* of Cameliard; wife of *Arthur* and Queen of Britain. In Welsh she was called 'Gwenhwyfar', sometimes translated as the 'White One', and described in the 'Triads' as one of the three great queens at Arthur's court, or as the triple Gwenhwyfar. In this early form, she appears to be an exemplar of the *Mothers*, the triple-goddess, or *Morrighan*. She may originally have been a form of *Sovereignty* — the early myth that she was abducted and married by *Mordred* so that he might rightfully rule Britain, indicates that he was trying to usurp Sovereignty by abducting her earthly manifestation. In later texts, Guinevere became solely the sinful and adulterous wife of Arthur, whose love of *Lancelot* causes the breakdown of the *Round Table*. She was also abducted by Meleagraunce and rescued by either Lancelot or Athur. In Malory, *Mordred* unmasked her adulterous love and set in motion the law which demanded her burning at the stake; this Arthur had to enforce as the arbiter of justice. She was rescued from the stake by Lancelot and taken to Joyous Gard in France. Arthur followed and laid siege to the castle. Eventually all parties were reconciled, by Guinevere becoming a nun in the monastery of Amesbury and by Lancelot's being banished from Britain. Lancelot attended her death-bed. [20, 72, 186]

Guinglain (A) *Gawain*'s son by the Lady *Ragnall* and hence his only legitimate offspring. There are traces in early Arthurian tradition of a lost story in which Guinglain featured, but all that is known of him now is that he became a Knight of the *Round Table* and was later killed by *Lancelot* when he was escaping from the Queen's chamber.

Guiromelant (A) Lover of *Gawain*'s sister *Clarissant*, who also hated her brother for killing his father but was unaware of their relationship. When Gawain is asked to carry a ring to Clarissant discoveries are made and a combat ensues. Gawain is persuaded not to kill his sister's *amor* and the story ends peacefully.

Guy of Warwick (L) A tenth-century legendary hero, said to have married the Earl of Warwick's daughter. He slew a monstrous *boar* and *cow* as well as a *dragon* who was about to devour a lion, which afterwards became his companion. He returned from the Holy Land to help King Ethelstan fight against the Danes and finally became a hermit.

Gwair/Gweir (W) The mysterious prisoner of the poem, 'Preiddeu Annwn': 'Perfect was the captivity in Caer Sidi/ According to the tale of *Pwyll* and *Pryderi*.' Gweir seems not to have been a personal name, but an alias or title which can be applied to the experiences of many characters within the 'Mabinogion', especially *Mabon*. He was said to have been released by *Goreu*. [17, 28, 80]

Gwalchmai (A) See *Gawain*.

Gwawl (W) The former betrothed of *Rhiannon*. He came as a suppliant to the feast where she was to be married to *Pwyll*, who granted all Gwawl might desire. Gwawl asked for both the feast and Rhiannon. At the wedding feast of Gwawl and Rhiannon, Pwyll likewise came disguised as a suitor and begged for his bag to be filled with food. Gwawl assented, but the bag was bottomless. Pwyll explained that it would never be filled until a nobleman pressed down the contents with his feet. This Gwawl did, becoming enclosed in the bag and beaten by Pwyll's men in a game called '*Badger* in the Bag' until he begged for mercy and relinquished Rhiannon. He was made to swear he would seek no revenge, but his maltreatment was avenged by his cousin, *Llwyd ap Cil Coed*. [17, 80]

Gwern (W) The son of *Branwen* and *Matholwch*. He was thrown in the fire by his uncle, *Efnissien*. [17, 80]

Gwion (W) See *Taliesin*.

Gwrach y Rhibyn (W) A form of Welsh *banshee*. Her name means 'Hag of the Warning'. She is nearer to the *Cailleach Bheare/Bheur* than the usual *Sidhe*-woman of Irish tradition. She always warns of a death and, like the *Washer at the Ford*, is often encountered at a crossroads or stream. [44]

Gwragedd Annwn (W) Lake maidens who endow fairy gifts on mortals and who occasionally marry men, with the proviso that they are never struck. One, like the French Melusine, started a dynasty of physicians who passed down their skills until the nineteenth century.

Gwyddno Garanhir (W) Father of *Elphin*. Many legends surround him, possibly stemming from a central lost tradition, since they seem to turn on one theme. He was the possessor of a magical container which could feed as many as took food from it (cf., *Thirteen Treasures of Britain*). His name is associated with a submerged kingdom in Cardigan Bay. The story of *Taliesin* tells how the *horses* of Gwyddno were poisoned by the *cauldron* of *Ceridwen* after *Gwion* had drained it of its goodness. [17, 28, 80]

Gwydion (W) Son of *Don* the Enchanter. He was steward to *Math*, his uncle, but abused his trust by causing war between Gwynedd and Dyfed on account of his brother, *Gilfaethwy*'s, lust for *Goewin*, the virgin footholder in whose lap Math rested his feet when he was not at war. The war was sparked off by Gwydion travelling in disguise to the court of *Pryderi* who had the only domesticated pigs, given to him by *Arawn*.

Gwydion made Pryderi part with them for *horses*, greyhounds and their trappings — all of which were made out of mushrooms and which returned to their own shapes the next day. The pigs were driven home and Pryderi's mèn pursued. In the ensuing combat Gwydion killed Pryderi while Gilfaethwy raped Goewin. The brothers were allowed no hospitality or shelter until they gave themselves up to Math who then turned Gwydion into.a stag, a sow, and a wolf, successively. Gwydion fathered offspring while in animal guise.

At the end of three years, both brothers were released from their punishment. When Math required a new footholder, Gwydion suggested his sister, *Arianrhod*, who submitting to a test of virginity bore two children — *Dylan* and *Llew*, the latter Gwydion raised and fostered. He enabled his protégé to overcome his mother's geise: to be nameless, weaponless and wifeless by means of his magic, and was helped by Math to make a wife out of flowers for Llew, *Blodeuwedd*. When the Flower-Bride betrayed Llew to his death, Gwydion searched for Llew's fetch — an *eagle* — and coaxed Llew back to life again. He cursed Blodeuwedd into *owl*-shape forever. [17, 80, 178]

Gwyglet (W) A hero of the Celtic epic 'The Goddoddin'. He joined the battle of Catreath (Catterick) and there fell to the lamentation of all. [190]

Gwynn ap Nudd (W) He leads the *Wild Hunt*. In Welsh legend he is the Lord of the Dead. He abducted *Creiddylad*, over whom he fought with *Gwythyr ap Greidawl*. According to the medieval legend of Saint *Collen*, Gwynn inhabited an otherworld kingdom whose gateway was *Glastonbury* Tor. [17, 80]

Gwythyr ap Greidawl (W) He was the intended husband of *Creiddylad*, but she was abducted by *Gwynn ap Nudd* whom he fought in perpetuity. Both men aided *Culhwch* and *Arthur* in achieving thirty-nine impossible tasks set by the giant in 'Culhwch and Olwen'. [17, 80]

H

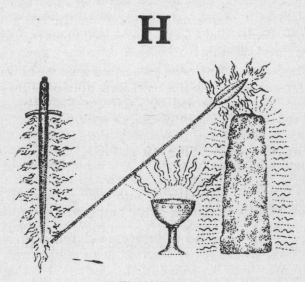

The Hallows

Hafgan (W) The otherworldly opponent of *Arawn* whom he was destined to fight every year. Arawn obligated *Pwyll* to fight his enemy for him, bidding him give but one blow since the second would revive him. Hafgan resembles closely the *Green Knight* and *Gromer Somer Joure*, the two opponents in *Gawain*'s story. [17, 25, 80]

Hallows (C) The kingly regalia or emblems of empowerment wielded by the king or hero, often the object of quest. The Hallows of Ireland were the Stone of Fal on which kings were inaugurated; the spear of *Lugh*, which gave victory in battle; the sword of *Nuadu*, which none could escape unwounded and the *cauldron* of *Dagda* from which no one came unsatisfied. These were brought from the Otherworld by the *Tuatha de Danaan*. *The Thirteen Treasures of Britain* represent a parallel tradition. The concept of the Hallows has been inherited by later traditions. Within folklore they are the pole of combat, the sword of light, the cauldron of cure and the stone of destiny. Magical tradition retains the four representative emblems of the elements: sword, spear, cup and pentacle. These emblems appear on orthodox tarot packs as the four suits. In Arthurian tradition they are: the Sword which is broken, the Spear of the *Dolorous Blow*, the Dish on which the head of the withdrawn *Grail* guardian is processed, and the Grail itself as a sacramental vessel or cauld-ron of plenty. The modern hallows exist as the regalia of the British monarch — the Sceptre or Rod of Equity and Mercy, the Swords of State, the Ampulla of Holy Oil and the Crown itself — replacing the ancient crowning stone as the primal symbol of *Sovereignty*. These items were guarded inviolate in the Tower of London, and have inherited an early sovereignty myth: that as long as the *ravens* never leave the Tower, Britain shall never be invaded. The Tower was once called the White Mount and was the place where *Bran*'s head was buried, to be a similar protection against invasion. It is his ravens which remain. [28, 38, 80, 83, 84]

Hare (B) The hare has long been associated with the power of trans-formation, and its strange movements were utilized in ancient modes of divination. This is recorded by Tacitus in his reports about the Icenian Revolt, during which *Boudicca* let a hare out of a fold in her cloak to see which way it ran preparatory to a battle. She has previously made sacrifices to the war-goddess *Andraste*, whose totem the hare may have been. [187]

Havelock the Dane (L) He was the true heir to the Danish throne but was ordered to be killed by Godard, the Usurper. He was taken by a fisherman, Grim, to England where Havelock became a byword and he was forcibly married to Princess Goldborough, the heir of King Athelstan, whose regent wished to humiliate her. Havelock came to Grimsby with his wife and she discerned the light shining from his mouth and the cross on his shoulder, and knew him to be of royal blood. He was eventually recognized and made king of England and Denmark. [143]

Hawk (B) In medieval times, the hawk, from kestral to *eagle*, was flown for sport. Celtic tradition records that the oldest animal was the Hawk of Achill, who tricked the eagle into giving up her warm nest in search of the answer to the question 'who can remember the coldest winter night?'. Although the *salmon* is normally con-sidered to be the oldest and wisest of beasts, the hawk was the oldest animal in this ancient oral tradition. *Gawain*'s ancient British name was Gwalchmai or Hawk of May. [80]

Hefaidd Hen (W) Father of *Rhiannon*. An underworld king who sponsored his daughter's betrothal to *Gwawl*. [17, 80]

Heimdal (N) Guardian of *Bifrost*, he was sent to guard the bridge to prevent the invasion of the *Frost Giants* into *Asgard*. The son of *Odin* and nine sea-maidens, Heimdal's hearing was so sensitive that he could hear grass growing on the earth or wool growing on the backs of sheep. He could also see a distance of one hundred miles by night both or day. He lived in the castle of Himinbiore and always wore shining white armour and carried a flashing sword. He also

possessed a magic horn Gjallarhorn, which could be heard throughout all the levels of heaven, earth and the Otherworld. It will summon
all the gods to battle when *Ragnarok* dawns. [53, 162]

Hel (N) The goddess who ruled the Underworld which was named
after her. She was the daughter of *Loki* and *Angrboda*. She was half-
black and half-white, and received all those who had died of disease
and old age into her kingdom. [53]

Hellawes (A) Enchantress. Lady of the Castle Nigramours (Necro-
mancy) who attempted to win the love of *Lancelot*, and failing to
do so, died.

Helyas (A) In the line of the *Grail Kings* he was fourth in line from
Celidoine, King of Scotland, from whose line in turn came both
Lancelot and *Galahad*.

Hereward the Wake (eleventh century) He held lands in Lincoln-
shire which were appropriated at the Conquest. He was said to have
fought a bear and a Cornish giant and to have won a magical suit
of armour. His resistance against William the Conqueror was mainly
carried out in the Fenlands, where Hereward holed up with other
disaffected men. His daring raids on Norman property and prowess
in ambush warfare won him renown. His death was unconfirmed
and it is possible that raids on the Normans persisted in his name
long after his death. [143]

Herla (L) A legendary British king who, according to Walter Map,
entered the underground kingdom of a dwarfish king who had goat's
hooves. They had an agreement that each would attend the other's
wedding. When Herla went to the underworld king's, he was given
a small bloodhound and told not to put it down until the dog leapt
down. He and his men rode back home and encountered a Saxon
shepherd who could just understand Herla's British speech. He knew
of stories of how Herla had disappeared underground, but that was
many hundreds of years ago. Some of Herla's host leapt down and
crumbled to dust, but Herla rides on waiting for the dog to leap
down. [32, 44]

Hermod (N) Messenger of the gods whom *Odin* sent to *Hel* to bring
back *Baldur*. Hel agreed only on condition that all the creatures of
the world weep at his loss. Only one failed to do so, an ancient hag
named Thok, who was almost certainly *Loki* in disguise. [7, 53]

Herne (L) The antler-horned spirit who haunts Windsor Great Park.
Like *Gwynn ap Nudd* and *Arawn*, he is said to lead the *Wild Hunt*
and be a conductor of the dead to the otherworldly regions. [88]

Heron (B) The heron shares the attributes and mythos of the *crane*
in many respects. [103]

Hesperides (G) The garden of the gods on the western extremity of the Greek world, in which the apples of fertility and growth grew, analogous with *Avalon, Fortunate Isles, Blessed Islands* etc. [57]

Hilda (ST) (614–80) Abbess of Whitby. She founded a double monastery and hosted the Synod of Whitby, at which Celtic and Roman Christians met to decide on liturgical matters. Although she favoured the Celtic faction, having herself organized her monastery after the Rule of Columbanus, she accepted the decision to universalize British practices and align them with Rome.

Caedmon became a monk under her influence, and was acclaimed the mother of the poor through her wisdom and generosity. She is said to have rid Eskdale of serpents by driving them off the edge of a cliff and cutting their heads off with a whip. The ammonites whose fossilized remains are to found at Whitby, are said to be the same serpents. Her feast-day is 17 November.

Hodur (N) God of Darkness, for which reason perhaps he was blind. Son of *Odin* and *Frigga*, and twin brother of *Baldur* whom he accidentally killed. As the gods were amusing themselves by throwing weapons at the invulnerable Baldur, *Loki* persuaded Hodur to throw a spear of mistletoe, knowing that this was the one thing which could harm him. Baldur's death was mourned by all but he could not be rescued from *Hel*. [53]

Hoenir (N) One of the creator gods who is said to have endowed the first humans with reason and understanding. After the battle between the *Aesir* and the *Vanir* he fled to *Vanaheim*. [53]

Horse (B) The horse is one of the primary totem beasts of the British Isles: a fact attested to by the taboo on eating horse-meat. The reverence in which the horse was held has not lessened over the centuries as a trip to any race-course will show. Horse-breeding and discussing the points of good racers or jumpers is still the common talk in any small Irish village. The White Mare was the mount of *Epona* or *Rhiannon*, goddesses associated powerfully with the horse, whose shape she often took. The most ancient horse chalk figure, White Horse Hill in Berkshire, still testifies to the joint Celtic and Saxon reverence for this animal. The horse with its magical bridle appears throughout folklore and Arthurian legend, where many knights go in quest for it, including *Gawain*. When found, the beast is usually a mare who turns back into a woman. [80]

Hugh (ST) (d.1255) Called Little Saint Hugh, to distinguish him from his fellow townsman Saint Hugh of Lincoln. His legend is typical of the anti-Jewish prejudice of the Middle Ages. He was a boy of nine who had been discovered in a well. The story circulated that he had been ritually murdered by the Jews. This led to anti-Semitic riots and persecution of the strong Jewish community of merchants in Lincoln. Miracles were attested at his shrine and, although not formally canonized, he was remembered on 27 August.

Hy Breasil (I) The Irish earthly paradise. It was considered to lie in the furthest west. Later Spanish adventurers who knew the myth applied it to the land they discovered — Brazil.

Hyperborea (G) The blessed realm governed by *Apollo*, believed by the Greeks to be located 'beyond the North Wind', possibly in Britain. *Abaris* was one of Apollo's priests. There was a yearly tribute sent to Delos from Hyperborea, to Apollo's shrine. Apollo's temple, described by Hecateus, is obviously intended as Stonehenge where, he writes, Apollo manifested himself to his followers every nineteen years. [57]

I

Iduna

Idun/Iduna (N) Goddess of spring who kept the gods eternally young with her golden apples of immortality. Lured out of *Asgard* by the wiles of *Loki*, Idun was recovered by him, at the insistence of the other gods. He took the form of a falcon and carried her off in his beak. She became the consort of Bragi, god of poetry. [53]

Igerna Igraine(A) Wife of *Gorlois of Cornwall*. She was loved by *Uther Pendragon*, who laid siege to Tintagil Castle and visited her disguised as her husband, with the help of *Merlin*. Gorlois was killed that night and, though she afterwards married Uther, he was uncertain as to the fatherhood of *Arthur* whom he put to fosterage with *Ector of the Forest Sauvage*. [20]

Illtyd (ST) (sixth century) Founder and Abbot of Llanwit Major. He was said to be a cousin of *Arthur* and visited his court, becoming a soldier until his conversion. All texts agree that he was the most learned Briton of his day. He was said to have been born in Brittany and his reputation credited him with being a magician. Lindsay suggests that his disciples demanded the old druidic right to exemption from taxes. He is remembered on 6 November.

Ing (N) A mysterious figure who is said to have appeared in a ship from across the sea. He founded the earliest race of Saxons and then vanished again eastwards. Some authorities number him among the *Aesir* and have suggested that his passage refers to the death voyage taken by heroes throughout the world.

Iollan (I) The son of *Fergus mac Roigh*. He went with his father to ask *Deirdre* and *Naoisi* to return to *Conchobar*; but they were ignorant that this was a false message, intended to entrap Deirdre and the Sons of *Usna*. Although Iollan defended them, Conchobar's champion, *Conall Cernach*, mortally wounded Iollan.

Irnan (I) She was one of three magical hag sisters who sought to enchant the *Fianna*. Irnan changed into the shape of a monster and challenged any of the troop to fight with her. *Fionn* accepted but *Goll* intervened and killed her.

Isolt of Ireland (A) Wife of *Mark* of Cornwall, for whom she was fetched from Ireland by her husband's nephew, *Tristan*. The two became lovers after drinking a love-potion, intended for the bridal couple, administered by *Brangaine*, Isolt's maid. Tristan and Isolt pursued their guilty love after her marriage to Mark, and then fled to the forest. Mark was eventually reconciled to Isolt when Tristan was banished from Cornwall. (This story parallels exactly the same course as that of *Diarmuid* and *Grainne* with *Fionn*, and of *Lancelot* and *Guinevere* with *Arthur*.) She died of a broken heart after arriving too late to save Tristan from a poisoned wound. She is also called Iseult or Isolde. [20, 136]

Isolt/Iseult of Brittany (A) *Tristan* married her after his banishment from Cornwall by *Mark*, believing *Isolt of Ireland* to be beyond his reach. She tricked him into believing that the other Isolt had not come to heal him from his wound, so that he died. [20, 136]

Ith (I) Son of *Bregon*. He sailed from Spain to arbitrate in a quarrel about the division of Ireland between three kings of the *Tuatha de Danaan*. So eloquent was his speech, that they feared he might seek to be king himself, and so he was killed. *Miled* set out to avenge his uncle. [15]

Iuchar (I) Brother of *Brian mac Tuirenn* who slew *Cian*, *Lugh*'s father.

Iucharba (I) Brother of *Brian mac Tuirenn*, who slew *Cian*, *Lugh*'s father.

J

Jack in the Green

Jack in the Green (L) The woodland spirit who, like the *Wood-Wose* or *Wild Herdsman*, guards the greenwood. He appears in many kinds of folk art, as a multi-foliate head peering through the leaves. Like the *Sheela na Gig*, he was especially portrayed in church decoration, usually as a roof-boss, where he was a constant reminder of earlier beliefs. [81]

Jaufre (A) See Griflet.

Jesus Christ Legend credits *Joseph of Arimathea* with bringing his young nephew, Jesus, to Britain in the course of one of his many trade-visits to these shores in search of Cornish tin. This is the source for William Blake's 'Jerusalem': 'And did those feet in ancient time/ Walk upon England's mountains green?' It is remarkable that all legends concerning Christ's connections with Britain should revolve around his youth and his death. The main relics of the Crucifixion were said to have been brought to *Glastonbury* by Joseph of Arimathea, thus establishing the Christian tradition and associations with the native *Grail* cult.

John Shorne (d.1313) He was a priest at Monks Risborough who was credited with conjuring the devil into a boot. He was not officially recognized as a saint, but a sufficient cult grew up to endow the chancel at North Maston church. He was patron of the blind, the unhappy and sufferers of toothache. His skill with devil-management was said to be the origin of jack-in-the-boxes.

Jormundgand (N) See *Midgard Serpent*.

Joseph of Arimathea (A) Traditionally, the uncle of Christ. He is said to have had connections with the Cornish tin trade and to have brought the young Jesus to Britain. Later, after the Crucifixion, he claimed the body of Christ and interred it in his own tomb. Imprisoned by the Romans, he was visited by the Risen Christ and entrusted with the secrets and guardianship of the *Grail*.

The Grail is variously understood as the cup of the Last Supper, or the two cruets of blood and sweat caught by Joseph at the Deposition from the Cross. Joseph was kept alive in prison by a dove which descended into the Grail with a wafer until he was released in the reign of Vespasian and travelled with his family to Britain, taking the Grail with him. He settled at *Glastonbury* and built the first Christian church of wattle. He planted his staff on Wearyall Hill where it burst into flower. A thorn tree still grows there today, and numerous scions grow in Glastonbury, although the original was chopped down during the English Civil War. It flowers at Christmas and is sent as a tribute to the Queen every year. [82, 86]

Jupiter (RB) The attributes of Jupiter as sky-god and wielder of thunderbolts became attached or associated with those of Celtic *Taranis*. Sky-columns were erected to Jupiter throughout the Celtic world — a native feature not found in classical Roman iconography. [59, 60]

K

Kentigern's Salmon

Kay/Cai/Cei/Keu (A) *Arthur*'s foster-brother: the son of *Ector of the Forest Sauvage*. He became the king's seneschal and was famed for his irascible and caustic tongue. In later versions, he is accused of the murder of Arthur's son, *Lohot*, although in the earliest Welsh versions he is among the first of Arthur's warriors, and a prodigious hero. Together with *Bedwyr* (*Bedivere*) he is nearly always present on the earliest adventures of Arthur. He rescued *Mabon* from imprisonment by bearing him out upon his back. [17, 20, 28, 80]

Kelpie (S) The Kelpie or *each-uisge* was a water-horse which could assume the shape of a man. He would lure riders on to his back and then dash away into a deep pool where they were drowned.

Kempe Owen (L) The hero who rescues a maiden enchanted into the shape of a *dragon* (see *Worm*) and who can only be disenchanted by being kissed three times. The step-mother in turn becomes a dragon, and is fated never to become human again until Saint Mungo (*Kentigern*) comes to Britain. [52, 94]

Kenneth/Cainnech (ST) (525–600) After plague struck his monastery in Ireland he came to Wales, and visited Scotland. He was an attractively forgetful character, visiting *Columba* with only one shoe on and forgetting his crozier on the beach. He nevertheless restored a dead girl to life and succoured her mother after both had been lost in the snow. He was said to have been close to animals in his hermetic period, though he had to admonish the birds to be quiet on Sundays, and expelled mice from his cell after they had eaten his shoes. He was something of a psychic, able to foretell coming events. His feast-day is 11 October.

Kentigern, Saint (S) The patron saint of Glasgow, from which he proselytized in Cumbria. Folklore makes him the grandson of *Urien* of Rheged. He and his mother were set adrift in a coracle but were miraculously saved. He vindicated the virtue of a queen who had given her ring to her lover: when the king demanded to see it, it was discovered in a *salmon*'s belly. The salmon is Kentigern's device. He was reputed to have baptized *Merlin* before his death. This last story is borrowed from the legend of *Suibhne Gelt*, who was confessed by Saint Moling after a life of paganism and madness.

Kirk, Robert (S) (1644–92) Author of 'The Secret Commonwealth', a treatise on Gaelic fairy tradition and second sight. He was a minister at Aberfoyle and made the first translation of the Bible into Gaelic. Although his tomb is shown, it is believed that he went into *Faery* and has not yet returned. Local women about to give birth try to ensure that they will have their child in his old house, because it is believed he will return from Faery reincarnated. [71, 113]

Kvasir (N) God of wisdom and poetic inspiration. He was created from the spittle of the *Aesir* and the *Vanir*, thus combining their knowledge. He went about the world teaching mankind and answering any questions he was asked. Eventually he was slain by two dwarves who coveted his wisdom and who made a drink from his blood which became an inspirational brew for poets. (See *Taliesin, Fionn* and *Cauldron*.) [53]

L

Lugh

Labraid (I) A king of *Mag Mell*, husband of *Liban*. He sent her to *CuChulainn* to beg for his help in battle; in return for this he gave him his sister, *Fand*. [12]

Labraid Longseach (I) He became dumb after having been made to eat his own father's heart by his uncle. He lived in exile until one day his speech returned while playing hurley. While in Gaul, he fell in love with *Moriath*, daughter of *Scoriath* the King. He employed *Craiftine* to play a sleep-inducing tune upon his harp and so slept Moriath, whom he married. He returned to Ireland and became King of Leinster. Like *Mark* of Cornwall, Labraid had horses' ears, for which he might have been deposed as a blemished king. He was successful in hiding this defect until his barber, though sworn to secrecy, told a tree, out of whose wood a harp was fashioned for Craiftine; it subsequently revealed the secret when played. [182]

Ladra (I) He was the pilot of *Cessair*'s ship and the only other man in that invasion of Ireland. He and his companion each shared the women between them, he with sixteen, the other with seventeen, which he considered an unjust division. However, he subsequently died from a surfeit of women, it was recorded.

Lady of the Fountain (A) Title of the mysterious countess in 'Yvain' by Chrétien de Troyes, and in 'The Lady of the Fountain' in the 'Mabinogion'. When her husband was killed by *Owain*, she demanded that Owain become her husband; by this means she could remain guardian of the fountain. [17, 80]

Lady of the Lake (A) An otherworldly woman who makes many appearances throughout the Arthurian cycle. As the Dame du Lac, she was *Lancelot*'s foster-mother. As *Nimue*, *Niniane* or *Vivienne*, she is the temptress who beguiled *Merlin* and succeeded in shutting him up under a stone or in a tree. Whilst in Malory's 'Le Morte d'Arthur' she gives *Arthur* his magic sword *Excalibur*. Behind all these personas stands a powerful exemplar of the Goddess, a figure of great antiquity who can be identified with Lady *Sovereignty*, since she guards the objects or *Hallows* of kingship. At the passing of Arthur, it is to her guardianship that *Bedivere* relinquishes Excalibur. Like the *Lady of the Fountain* and the damsels who guard the wells in the story of *Amangons*, she is the otherworld empowerer of kings. [20, 23]

Lailoken (C) Scottish prophet and madman, whose life is a major source for that of Merlin. His story is contiguous with *Suibhne Gelt* also.

Lambton Worm (L) The beast was said to live in a well near Lambton Castle in County Durham. It ravaged the district until killed by Lord Lambton's son, who dressed in armour covered with razors. The *worm* wrapped itself about him and was killed. This advice was given by a witch who, in return, made him swear to kill the first thing he saw on his return. Instead of a *dog*, as arranged, he met his father and refused to kill him. The witch cursed the family which resulted in each of them having a violent end. (See *Worms*.) [120]

Lamorack de Galles (A) Son of King *Pellinore*. Knight of the *Round Table*, he ranked only a little below *Lancelot*. He became the lover of *Morgause* and was killed by her sons, *Gawain*, *Gaheris* and *Agravaine* because he had killed their father. [20]

Lance of Longinus (A) See *Grail Lance*.

Lancelot du Lac (A) The greatest knight of Arthurian Britain, unbeaten by anyone except his son, *Galahad*. The son of King Ban of Benoic in France, he was a prince in his own right. He was fostered by the *Lady of the Lake* and prepared by her to support *Arthur* and the concept of the *Round Table*. He was none the less flawed, being unable to overcome his love of *Guinevere*, Arthur's queen. Because of this sin, he failed to achieve the *Grail*, though he later achieved the miracle of healing a knight called Sir Urrey of Hungary, whom only the best knight in the world could heal.

Lancelot was indeed the strongest man but he never achieved the heights of spiritual chivalry. He slew his greatest friend, *Gareth* of Orkney, by accident while rescuing Guinevere from the stake. After the departure of Arthur he retired to a hermitage and became a holy man. He died and was buried at his castle, Joyous Gard, possibly Alnwick in Northumberland. Although Lancelot appears late in the Arthurian corpus, he is none the less present, in prototype, in the persons of *Llew, Lugh* and *Llwch Llawwyanawc*. [20, 23, 84]

Launfal/Lanval (A) Arthurian knight who married a fairy woman and then boasted of her beauty when *Guinevere* made advances to him. In this way he broke a promise of silence and lost his love. This theme appears in the stories of *Macha* and *Edric*. It probably is derived from the story of the French fairy mistress, Melusine, which acts as a prototype for many of these fairy liaisons.

Lavaine (A) Son of Sir Bernard of Astolat and brother to *Elaine* le Blanke and Sir Tirre. He is befriended by *Lancelot*, who also knights him and in time he becomes one of the finest of the *Round Table Knights*. At the time of Lancelot's arraignment for the love of *Guinevere* he accompanies his master to France and is raised to be the Duke of Arminak.

Leanan Sidhe (I) The Fairy Mistress who encounters poets and musicians inspiring them with her muse-like power. She appears frequently in Irish poetic tradition as the central figure of the *Aisling* or vision, in which the poet meets her on a hillside. The music and poetry which she inspires is usually indicative of otherworldly sadness and regret for the past glories of Ireland.

Lear (L) King of Britain, son of *Bladud*. In his old age he gave away parts of his kingdom as dowries to his daughters, in proportion to the amount of affection they said they felt for him. Goneril and Regan both flattered him, but *Cordelia* gave an honest answer, for which she was cast out, with no dowry. Both Goneril and Regan gradually stripped him of his retinue until he had only one retainer, whereupon he fled to Cordelia in France. He regained his kingdom with her help but died. Cordelia had him buried 'in a four-sided grave' on the banks of the Soar, in a chamber dedicated to Janus, to which craftsmen made pilgrimage on the first day of the year. Lear is the same as *Llyr*. Shakespeare's play follows the general course of the story. [9]

Lebharcham (I) The female messenger or runner attached to the court of *Conchobar mac Nessa*. She was also the foster-mother of *Deirdriu*.

Leodegrance (A) King of Cameliard, father of *Guinevere*. One of the earliest supporters of *Arthur* in his wars against the rebellious kings. [20]

Leprechaun (I) He is a folk-variant of the *Fir Dhearga* or the Red Men and, like them, indulges in jokes at mortals' expense. He is often the guardian of a treasure though, in the way of things, he rarely allows mortal adventurers to get the better of him. The modern leprechaun is almost totally obliterated under a welter of cute Irish green-wash and has been devalued for tourist use.

Liadin (I) She was a poet whom *Cuirithir* fell in love with. He remarked that a child of their union would be famous, which offended her so much that she forsook poetry and became a nun. Cuirithir then became a monk. Both regretted their hasty action and, though they loved each other until death, they were never again united in the flesh. The cycle of poems telling of their pain and love is as touching and bitter as that correspondence between the tragic lovers, Abelard and Heloise.

Liban (I) Wife of *Labraid*. She acts as a messenger between the early realms and those of *Mag Mell* in order to induce *CuChulainn* to help her husband. CuChulainn sent *Loegaire* ahead to reconnoitre first. [12]

Lionel (A) *Round Table Knight*, brother to *Bors* and cousin of *Lancelot*.

Lios Alfar (N) See *Alfar*.

Lir/Ler (I) The father of *Manannan*. By his wife *Aobh*, he had four children: *Fionnuala, Aed, Conn* and *Fiachra*. When Aobh died, he married her sister, *Aoife* who turned his children into *swans*. Aoife played both father and children off against each other so that Lir thought his children unfilial, but he eventually learned what had been done to them. He went at last to the *Sidhe* where *Bodh Dearg* was king and bade him punish his foster-child, Aoife. He is analogous with *Lear* and *Llyr*. The story of father and seemingly ungrateful children is remarkably persistent throughout this strand of the myth. [13]

Llacheu (A) *Arthur*'s illegitimate son by Lysanor, according to ancient Welsh texts. Nothing is known of him except for a later medieval story which tells of his murder by *Kay*. His head was sent to Arthur and *Guinevere* in a wooden casket. he is also called Borre or Boare in other versions or *Lohot*. [28]

Llamrei (A) *Arthur*'s white mare in early Welsh sources.

Llassar Llaes Gyfnewid (W) A giant who lived under a lake in Ireland and emerged bearing the *cauldron* of rebirth on his back. His wife, Cymidei Cymeinfoll, was twice as big as he and bore a child every six weeks. Within six more weeks each child was as big as a fully-

armed warrior. *Matholwch* took them both in but soon grew tired
of them and had the whole family confined in an iron house which
was then heated from without. Only Llassar and his wife escaped
with the cauldron, which they then gave to *Bran*, with whom they
settled peaceably. [17, 80]

Llefelys (W) Son of *Beli*. He was made King of France, according
to legend. (See *Lludd*.)

Llew Llaw Gyffes (W) Son of *Arianrhod* and an unknown father.
He was born as a result of his mother's submitting to a test of
virginity. Being incompletely mature, he was incubated by *Gwydion*,
his uncle, who raised him. He was taken on subsequent occasions
to his mother, to be given a name and weapons, each of which she
refused, cursing him with namelessness and lack of arms.

Disguising both himself and the boy, Gwydion decoyed Arianrhod
into exclaiming on the boy's dexterity with the sling: 'With what
a skilful hand the fair one hit the bird!' which gave Llew his name.
He then raised a phantom army against her castle whereupon she
armed her own son, who was disguised as a bard. She also cursed
him with the fate of having no wife of earthly lineage.

This was overcome by Gwydion and *Math*, who formed
Blodeuwedd out of blossom and gave her to Llew. She soon betrayed
him and fell in love with *Gronw Pebr*, with whom she planned Llew's
death. She coaxed the circumstances of Llew's fated death from her
husband. He could only be killed by a spear which was forged for
a year only during the mass on Sunday; he could not be killed inside
nor outside; neither on horse nor on foot. When Gronw had forged
the spear, she made Llew show her how impossible such a death
would be. He had constructed a roofed bath-tub on a river-bank and
brought a billy-goat alongside so that he stood with one foot on the
bath and one on the goat. Gronw was able to throw his spear and
kill Llew. But Llew's spirit flew off in the shape of an *eagle* and was
coaxed back into his body by Gwydion.

Llew is the Welsh counterpart of *Lugh* and may be a precursor of
Lancelot. He is associated with shoemakers (since he was so disguised
by Gwydion) and with the Spear or Sword of Light, one of the
Hallows. [17, 20, 76, 80]

Lludd (W) Son of *Beli*, brother to *Llefelys*. He was King of Britain
and rebuilt London Town, which is named after him. Three plagues
came upon Britain: a race called the Coranians who knew whatever
was spoken; a shriek which was heard on May-Eve and which
blighted crops, killed animals and children and made women barren;
and the disappearance of the King's provisions. Lludd sought the
counsel of *Llefelys*, who told him that the Coranians could be
overthrown by their drinking an infusion of crushed insects in water;

that the shriek was caused by *dragons* who were trapped at the exact centre of Britain, and who could be overcome by strong mead then buried there; and that the thief of the provisions was a man of power who cast sleep on the court and stole the food. Lludd overcame all three.

The story of the dragons is analogous to those in *Merlin*'s story, while the thief of the provisions is perhaps associated with *Gwyddno Garanhir*. The three plagues upon Britain reflect the enchantments which fall upon a kingdom in the reign of an unworthy king. (See *Wasteland*.) [17]

Llwch Llawwyanawc/Lleminawc/Llenllawc (W) The Welsh warrior who accompanied *Arthur* on his raid on *Annwn* to gain the *Hallows*. His shining sword (the Sword of Light or Arthur's *Caledfwlch*) cleared the way before the great *cauldron*, enabling it to be taken. He is analogous with *Lugh*, *Llew* and *Lancelot*. [17, 80, 84]

Llwyd ap Cil Coed (W) The cousin of *Gwawl*. He set the land of Dyfed under an enchantment and spirited away both *Pryderi* and *Rhiannon* to a period of servitude in the Underworld. He was defeated by *Manawyddan*. [17, 80]

Llyr (W) The father of *Manawyddan*, *Bran*, *Branwen*, *Efnissien* and *Nissien*, according to 'Branwen, Daughter of Llyr'. His name means 'of the sea'. He is cognate with the Irish *Lir* and King *Lear* of Geoffrey of Monmouth and Shakespeare. He is said to be one of the three notable prisoners of Britain in the 'Triads'. He is also called Lludd Llaw Ereint (Silver Hand), analogous to *Nuadu* and *Nodens*. [17, 28, 80]

Loathly Lady (C) The figure of the hag, *cailleach* or Loathly Lady is widespread in Celtic literature from early times up to the Arthurian cycle. Her appearance in these later stories attests to the persistent tradition of *Sovereignty*, who is the personification of the land and in whose gift lies its kingship. She appears to the kingly-candidate as a hag of hideous appearance and asks him to kiss her: his acceptance as king is thus shown, since he is willing to embrace all that kingship entails, and the Loathly Lady becomes a fair maiden once more, becoming his consort.

In later Arthurian tradition, she appears as the *Grail* messenger: *Sovereignty* disguised as a hag who walks the land, guiding and testing the Grail candidate. She rebukes *Perceval* for failing to ask the *Grail Question*. She appears as *Ragnell* and marries *Gawain* (*Arthur*'s champion and heir), helping Arthur to successfully answer the question 'What is it women desire most?' — the answer being Sovereignty (diminished to 'her own way' in later versions). In *Parzival* she becomes *Cundrie* in whom her capacity for wisdom is most marked. (See *Niall of the Nine Hostages*.) [3, 14, 26, 83, 186]

Locrinus (L) Eldest son of *Brutus*. He ruled over Loegria or England. He fell in love with Estrildis, daughter of the King of Germany, forsaking his wife *Guendolena* who subsequently defeated him in battle. His name is the basis for the name of England which is used in Arthurian legend and in modern Welsh: Loegres or *Logres*. [9]

Loegaire (I) He was *CuChulainn*'s charioteer and, with him, was one of the heroes whom *Bricriu* baited at his feast. he visited *Mag Mell* and there rescued its queen, *Fiachna*'s wife from abductors. In reward, Loegaire was given Sun-Tear for his wife. He remained in the Otherworld for a year before becoming homesick. Fiachna gave him a horse on which to return home but before he dismounted, he realized how much better was Mag Mell. In a variant text, he stopped a spear intended for CuChulainn and died. [12]

Logres (A) One of the earliest names for Arthurian Britain, deriving from *Locrinis*, son of Brut. It remains the name for the 'inner' Britain as the secret heart of the land. [4, 24, 26, 83]

Lohot (A) See *Llacheu*.

Loki (N) The trickster god of the *Aesir*. Said by some to be the son of Bestla, *Odin*'s brother, and to have assisted in the making of the first human beings. Later he became a darker figure, whose hatred of *Baldur* brought about the death of this beloved god. His first wife was Glut, by whom he had two daughters. His second wife, the giantess *Angrboda*, bore him *Hel, Fenris* and the *Midgard Serpent*. Eventually he became so troublesome that the gods caught and bound him in a cavern beneath the earth, guarded by a great serpent whose venom fell upon him. His agonized struggles caused earthquakes. At the end of the age of gods, *Heimdal* will kill him. [7, 53]

Lot/Lotha (A) King of Lothian and Orkney in the Arthurian story. Husband of *Morgause* and father of *Gawain, Gaheris, Agravaine* and *Gareth*. He was killed by King *Pellinore* in one of the early battles for the crown of Britain, since Lot opposed *Arthur*. This led to a feud between his sons and those of Pellinore. [20]

Lovel (A) *Gawain*'s second illegitimate son by the unnamed sister of Bradiles. Nothing is known of his career except that, together with his brother, he was killed by *Lancelot* when they joined *Mordred* in an attempt to capture Lancelot in the Queen's chamber.

Lucan the Butler (A) The first and last of *Arthur*'s trusted men, Lucan became Butler to the King at his crowning and retained the post throughout his reign. He eventually became a knight of the *Round Table* and was present at the last battle of *Camlan*. There he received a wound which killed him when he later tried to help

Bedivere carry the wounded Arthur away from the field of battle. He is sometimes described as Bedivere's brother. [20]

Lud (L) See also *Lludd*. He was the eldest brother of Cassivelaunus. He renamed Trinovantum as Caer Lud or Caerlundein, later called London. He was buried near a gateway in the capital called Porthlud or Ludgate. [9]

Lugaid (I) Son of *Cu Roi* and *Blanaid*. He was known as the 'Son of Three Dogs' because Blanaid was believed to have lain with *Conall Cernach* and *CuChulainn* as well as her husband (Cu or Conn means *dog*). He gave the death blow to CuChulainn but as he struck off his head, the sword fell and cut off his own hand. Conall Cernach avenged CuChulainn's death by fighting Lugaid in single combat, during which, for fairness, he agreed to have one hand tied behind his back. [12]

Lugh (I) The grandson of *Balor*, born of *Ethniu* and *Cian*, and fostered by *Manannan* and *Tailtiu*. He was the guardian of the spear of Gorias which killed all opponents. When the *Tuatha de Danaan* were oppressed by the *Fomorians*, he came to their aid. He was refused entrance to the hall of their king, *Nuadu*, but eventually was allowed in because he combined many skills in one person, for which he was called Samildanach (Many-Skills). He became the Tuatha's substitute king in place of Nuadu who was a blemished or *Wounded King* because he had lost his hand in battle. After Nuadu's death, Lugh himself became the Tuatha's rightful king. He killed his grandfather Balor by piercing him through his baleful eye. He was the spiritual father of *CuChulainn*, and fought in his son's place in order to give him rest during his lone combat at the ford.

Lugh is analogous to *Llew* and to the warrior *Llwch Llawwynawc* who helped *Arthur* obtain the *cauldron* from *Annwn*. His mythos passed partially into that of *Lancelot*. His many epithets describe him as being skilful with weapons and crafts. Everything about him is of the light and of the victorious sun over darkness. [5, 15, 80, 149]

Lughnasadh (C) Celebrated on 1 August, this Celtic festival marked the season of harvest. Although it is named after the god, *Lugh*, its origins are more closely associated with Lugh's foster-mother, *Tailtiu*, who laboured to clear the plains of Ireland for agrarian use and so died. Sacred games were held in her honour at Teltown and temporary marriages were lightly entered into, with no binding contract, though many such unions endured. Farm-hands were hired and animals sold at this time. The reason for attaching Lugh's name to this feast is presumably due to his association with the goddess of *Sovereignty*, with whom he mystically entered into marriage and with whom he ruled from the Otherworld. Tailtiu was clearly a type of the Goddess of the Land.

Lunet/Luned/Linet (A) In 'Yvain' by Chrétien de Troyes and 'Lady of the Fountain' in the 'Mabinogion', she is the servant of the *Lady of the Fountain* who frequently rescues the hero from death and who appears to be possessed of magical powers. She is in turn rescued from imprisonment under a stone by *Owain/Yvain*. [4, 17]

Lyonesse (A) The lost lands off the coast of Cornwall, birthplace of *Tristan*. Memories of *Atlantis* are woven into this drowned land.

M

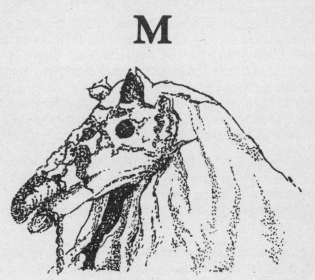

Mari Lwyd

Mab (L) The Queen of *Faery*. The etymology of the name is uncertain, although it has been suggested that it may be associated with *Maeve* or the Welsh 'mab' for baby, since she is called the 'fairies' midwife'.

Mabon (W) The son of *Modron*. He was one of the famous prisoners of Britain according to the 'Triads'. The story of his loss and discovery is told in 'Culhwch and Olwen'. He was stolen from between his mother and the wall when he was three nights old. From the context of the story it is obvious that this happened at the beginning of time. He is only found in his prison at Gloucester by *Cai* and *Bedwyr* after they have questioned many beasts and birds, each of whom leads them on to the *salmon* who knows of his hiding place.

Mabon is the Wondrous Youth of Celtic tradition: like *Merlin*, he is the child of otherworld and earthly parents. His cult was widespread in north-west Britain, along Hadrian's Wall. He shares many of the aspects of Greek *Apollo*: as hunter and harper, he appears in many inscriptions on Romano-British dedications. Like *Angus*, he is the god of youth. His name merely means 'son' and so is a mystery title which is ascribable to many suitable local deities. [17, 28, 80]

Macha (I) An aspect of the *Morrighan*. Macha herself appeared in three guises: Macha, wife of Nemed; Macha the Red, and Macha, wife of *Crunnchu*. The last mentioned was the silent wife of a farmer who came from the Otherworld. She imposed one condition upon her husband — that he should not mention her to anyone.

The king boasted that his *horses* were the swiftest but Crunnchu said that Macha was faster. She was made to run a circuit against the horses when she was about to give birth. She won the race, and after delivering her two children, cursed Ulster saying that when its greatest need was upon it, all its warriors would suffer the weakness of a woman in childbirth for five days and four nights, to the ninth generation. It was so that *CuChulainn* defended Ulster single-handed, because he was not descended from the stock of Ulster. Emain Macha (the Twins of Macha) was named after her. Macha the Red was the battle-aspect of the Morrighan and it was upon the Pole of Macha that the heads of slaughtered men were stuck. [5, 27, 80]

Madoc ap Owain Gwynedd (W) A Welsh prince who discovered America in the twelfth century. Southey wrote a long poem about this legend. George Catlin, the nineteenth-century artist who lived among the Indians of the Mid-West, found supposed traces of European ancestors among their customs.

Mador de la Porte (A) Cousin of Sir Patrice, a knight who was murdered, his death blamed on *Guinevere*. In fury and anguish at his cousin's death he challenges the knights who defend the Queen, but fortunately the real culprit is discovered and slain by *Lancelot*, and Guinevere willingly forgives her would-be accuser. [20]

Madrun/Matriana (ST) (fifth century) She was said to be the daughter of Vortimer, *Vortigern*'s son who fled with her son Ceidio, from Caerwent to Cornwall where she died. Her story may be vaguely derived from the lost myth of *Modron*. Madrun is depicted fleeing from battle carrying her son. Her feast-day is 9 April.

Maelduine (I) The son of a nun who was raped by his father, *Ailill*. He desired to go in search of his father's murderers, and so made a skin-boat and sailed on a great voyage among the *Blessed Islands*, where he encountered many islands, including *Tir na mBan*, where he and his crew would have stayed, but for their homesickness for Ireland. (See *Bran* and *Brendan*.) Many of the islands are similar to those visited by Brendan. [19, 98]

Maeve/Medb (I) Queen of Connacht. She was originally the woman of *Conchobar* whom she left for *Ailill*. She coveted the Brown *Bull* owned by the Ulsterman Daire. When he refused to give it to her she appointed the disaffected Ulster warrior, *Fergus mac Roigh* to attack Ulster. They succeeded in their attempt to raid the Bull because the Ulstermen were suffering from the debility brought upon them by *Macha*'s curse. Only *CuChulainn* was able to hold the ford against them and he was eventually killed by the help of the daughters of *Calatin*. Maeve was renowned for her lust for men, taking her lovers indiscriminately. In antiquity she may have represented the earthly *Sovereignty* in her own person. [5, 12, 27]

Mag Mell (I) The pleasant plain in which gods and immortal heroes lived and sported. *Manannan* speaks of it to *Bran mac Febal* as the 'plains' of the sea wherein otherwordly folk move as on land: its fish are its flocks, its vegetation are its forests, while its chariots are ships. [19]

Mag Mor (I) The great plain: the heartland of the gods where men and maidens lived together without shame, where music always sounded, where possessions were unknown and where the ale was more intoxicating than the best produced in Ireland.

Magnus (ST) (1075-1116) Earl of Orkney. When King Magnus Barefoot of Norway invaded Orkney, Magnus fled to Scotland, returning when the king died. However, his cousin Haakon was in possession of Orkney. The rival earls decided to divide the islands between them. After a few years of uneasy peace, a conference was called on Egilsay, each earl bringing an equal shipload of retainers. It was clear that Haakon intended to murder Magnus, and Haakon's cook, Lifolf, was bidden to strike the blow. Magnus is remembered on 16 April. [163]

Maledisant (A) Wife of *Bruno le Noir* (La Cote Mail-Taile) who begins by accompanying him on a dangerous adventure rebuking him mercilessly all the time for his ragged and ill-fitting clothes and apparent lack of money. In the end she falls in love with him, and perhaps as the similar tale of *Gareth* and *Linet* should have ended, marries him. Her name, which means 'ill speech' clearly reflects her acid tongue.

Manannan mac Lir (I) The sea-deity of Ireland, older than the *Tuatha de Danaan*, although he is reckoned as one of them. He prepared the *Sidhe* for their occupation after the coming of the sons of *Miled*. He was the foster-father of many gods, including *Lugh*. He lost his wife, *Fand* to *CuChulainn*. He became the father of *Mongan*, his earthly incarnation, by visiting Caintigerna in the shape of her husband, *Fiachna*.

He is the guardian of the *Blessed Islands*: these have been identified with the Isle of Arran (Emain Abhlach) and the Isle of Man. In his crane-bag, he kept the earliest forms of the *Hallows*, including his magical coracle and the cup of truth, which *Cormac* journeyed to find. In the Irish version of Nennius, Manannan is mentioned as one of the *Grail* guardians with *Pryderi*. He was a great shape-shifter and night-visitor of women, often assuming the shape of a sea-bird or *heron*. He is analogous to *Manawyddan*. [5, 15, 19]

Manawyddan (W) Son of *Llyr*. He is the Welsh equivalent of *Manannan*. He was left landless on the death of *Bran* and became the husband of *Rhiannon*. He helped break the enchantments upon Dyfed, caused by *Llwyd* in revenge for *Gwawl*'s rough treatment at the hands of Rhiannon's first husband, *Pwyll*. Manawyddan is a man of cunning and a master craftsman, able to earn his own living when the land is enchanted. As instructor and man of power, he stands in the place of father to *Pryderi*, and inherits the qualities of Pwyll. [17, 28, 80]

Maponus (RB) Analogous with *Mabon*. Dedications to him occur as far apart as Gaul and Dumfriesshire. He assimilated the attributes of *Apollo* and appears on a relief with *Diana*, who is likely to have taken on the attributes of *Modron* in that locality. [60, 80, 103]

March (A) See *Mark*.

Mari Lwyd (W) A hobby-horse made of a garlanded horse-skull which is borne about at Christmas-time. Its bearers try to gain entrance to each house it visits by means of a riddling dialogue song: the occupants have to cap the lines which the Mari sings, if they are unable to, the Mari Lwyd enters and her bearers are given refreshment. The ritual custom is based on a legend which says that the Mari Lwyd was put out of the stable in which Christ was born and that she wanders the land in search of a place to stay. It is possibly associated with the cult of *Epona* and *Rhiannon*. [80]

Mark (A) King of Cornwall, husband of *Isolt of Ireland* who betrayed him for love of *Tristan*. He appears in Welsh tradition as March who had horses' ears. He unknowingly slept with *Brangaine* on his wedding night, not with Isolt — a ruse to deceive him that he had a virgin wife. [20, 136]

Marrok (A) Said to be a knight who was also a werewolf, having lost his human shape for many years through the evil of his wife. She, it seems, discovered his secret, and he had to hide his clothes until he was ready to turn back into a human being. She stole them and Marrok was a wolf for many years until *Arthur* discovered him behaving in a very unwolf-like manner and brought him home.

Here the wolf was gentle with all save his wife and her lover. She was then forced to confess and Marrok was given back his clothing, whereupon he returned to his natural shape. It is made clear that he was not the kind of werewolf normally written about, but simply a man who, perhaps under enchantment, turned into a wolf at night.

Mars (RB) He was a particularly popular god in Roman Britain, with both native and occupying peoples alike, so that his name appears linked with that of native deities embodying similar characteristics, e.g. Mars Loucetius (Brilliant), or Mars Rigonemetis (King of the Sacred Grove). Mars forsakes his classical attributes, reverting instead of the original Italian attributes as a god of vegetation and agriculture. In Britain he is also associated with healing and sometimes appears as the Triple Mars — a truly Celtic idea — complete with ram-headed snakes, the attributes of *Cernunnos*. He is often partnered by *Nemetona*. [59, 103]

Mary, the Blessed Virgin England has been traditionally known as Mary's Dowry for centuries. The claim to this title is not difficult to discover, since *Joseph of Arimathea* founded the first Christian church at *Glastonbury* — a humble edifice of wattles which was dedicated to Our Lady Mary. He was also, according to variant legends, supposed to have brought Mary with him to England after the death and resurrection of her son. The other focus of her cult was at Walsingham where in 1061, Lady Richeldis had a vision of Mary which commanded her to build a replica of Mary's house in Nazareth.

This shrine became the pilgrimage centre of England up until the Reformation when the image of the Virgin was destroyed. The shrine is now operative again and drawing almost as many pilgrims as in the Middle Ages where its reputation for answering prayer has not failed. The healing well still dispenses its waters. The Milky Way became known as the Walsingham Way.

Math (W) Son of *Mathonwy* and uncle to *Gwydion*, *Gilfaethwy* and *Arianrhod*. He was omniscient and full of wisdom, a great king. In 'Math, Son of Mathonwy', he can only live when his feet are in the lap of a virgin footholder, *Goewin*. War causes him to abandon this mode of living temporarily and Goewin is raped by Gilfaethwy. He marries her, to assuage her shame, and punishes his nephews, Gilfaethwy and Gwydion, by causing them to assume various animal disguises. It is with his help that Gwydion makes *Blodeuwedd* out of flowers, as a bride for *Llew*, his great-grandson. [17, 28, 80]

Matholwch (W) King of Ireland who married *Branwen* and ill-treated her. He was defeated and deposed in favour of his son, *Gwern*, by *Bran*. [17, 80]

Matres (RB) See the *Mothers*.

Maxen Wledig (W) The Welsh name for the Emperor Magnus Maximus (AD 383-8). In the 'Dream of Maxen', the Emperor dreams of an unknown woman with whom he falls in love. Messengers eventually report her existence in Wales so that he leaves Rome in order to marry her. She is *Elen*. The historical Maximus, underlying the legend, did indeed serve in Britain, but took many troops away from the island in his struggles against his rival Western Emperor, Gratian, thus leaving Britain unprotected. Traces of fact remain in the legend: the Welsh retained his name where it appears in many genealogies of noble families as an imperial connection. [17, 28]

Mechi (I) He was the *Morrighan*'s son. He was killed by *Ogma*'s son, because of a prophecy which said that he would ruin Ireland. This was due to his three hearts out of which three serpents would hatch, devastating the land. [5]

Meleagraunce (A) See *Melwas*.

Melkin (W) A prophet and poet who predated *Merlin*. He left a prophecy concerning the burial place of *Joseph of Arimathea* and the objects which he brought to *Glastonbury*. Apart from an entry in the Annals of Glastonbury Abbey, evidence is scanty for his existence, but there is a strong indication that he embodied an ancient tradition before Christian times.

Melwas (A) The otherworld king who abducted *Guinevere*. In the ancient 'Life of Caradoc', the saint mediates between *Arthur* and Melwas (here called the King of the Summer Country) to prevent warfare between them. In later medieval tradition, Melwas becomes Sir Meleagraunce and it is *Lancelot*, rather than Arthur, who is the rescuer. [72]

Mercury (RB) He was particularly popular among natives of Britain and, although he retained his classical attributes, he blended in well with native gods. He is shown with caduceus, cockerel and purse, indicating his function as conductor of the dead and god of financial transactions. He is partnered by *Rosmerta* in many inscriptions and reliefs. [59, 103]

Merlin/Merlinus/Myrddyn (A) Arch-mage of Britain; chief adviser and guardian of *Arthur*; magician, shaman and mystagogue. Merlin's origins are uncertain. He was originally called Myrddyn in British, but Geoffrey of Monmouth, whose 'Historia Regnum Brittaniae' and 'Vita Merlini' are the chief sources for his life, renamed him Merlin. In these books Merlin makes a series of prophecies concerning the fate of Britain.

It is possible that he may be the same character as the sixth-century Welsh poet, Myrddyn, several of whose poems are still extant. (He fought on the side of King Gwenddolau against *Rhydderch Hael* at Arfderydd in AD 575 and went mad as a result of losing the battle.) The madness of Merlin is contained in several traditional stories concerning *Suibhne Gelt* and *Lailoken*. All three mad prophets are said to suffer the threefold death caused by falling, hanging and drowning, although the usual tale of Merlin's death or passing away became attached to the story of *Niniane* or *Vivienne*, an otherworld woman who tricked him into revealing his magic. She then shut him up in a glass tower, or under a stone or in a hawthorn tree. This tradition is probably a garbled understanding of Merlin's withdrawal from the world into *Faery* or the Otherworld.

The French tradition speaks of his 'esplumoir' or 'moulting-cage' where he is supposed to abide, derived from the two meanings of his name: *hawk* or man of the sea. His early career sees him as a child of an otherworldly father or daemon and an earthly woman. *Vortigern*'s tower, which kept falling down, could only be built if the foundations were sealed by the blood of a child without a father.

The boy Merlin Emrys (*Ambrosius*) was found but he refuted the druids of Vortigern, by stating that the tower was built over the chest in which two *dragons* — one red and one white — quarrelled continually. He made his prophecies when the foundations were uncovered to reveal the dragons, which represent the two races of Britains and Saxons. He was said to be the guardian of the *Thirteen Treasures of Britain*, which he kept in his glass tower on Bardsey Island. He is the tutelar of Britain which is anciently called Clas Merdin or Merlin's Enclosure. [9, 29, 110, 111, 112]

Merrow/Murdhuacha (I) The Irish form of the mermaid. They usually appear before storms and traditionally inter-married with mortals. Some families claimed descent from them, showing webbed hands and feet as proof of these ancestral unions. (See *Seal*.) [47]

Mess Buachalla (I) The daughter of *Etain* and Cormac, King of Ulster. Cormac, tiring of Etain, bade her baby daughter be cast into a pit, but she was rescued and fostered by the cowherds of Eterscel, King of Tara. When she grew up she was kept closely guarded by the cowherds, but Esterscel saw her and desired her. It was prophesied that a woman of unknown race would bear him a son, but Mess Buachalla — the Cowherds' Fosterchild, as she was known — was warned by an otherworldly man in the shape of a bird; it was he who was the real father of *Conaire*, not Eterscel. [6]

Miach (I) After his father *Diancecht* made a silver hand for *Nuadu*, Miach, whose skill surpassed his, made a hand of flesh instead. In his jealous rage Diancecht wounded him in three separate attacks, which Miach healed. On the fourth attack he received a wound in the brain from which he died. 365 herbs grew from his grave which his sister Airmed gathered, but Diancecht confused them so that no one knew which was which. [5]

Midgard Serpent (N) Also called *Jormundgand*. The monstrous son of *Loki* and *Angrboda*. He grew until his body encircled the earth and he could capture his own tail. Placed in the sea by *Odin*, he writhed so as to cause tempests. He will only be destroyed by *Ragnarok.* [53]

Midir (I) King of the *Sidhe* of Femen. He lost his wife *Etain* and went in search of her to the court of *Eochaid Airem*, whom she had married. He sought her through many reincarnations and strove to remind her of their happiness within the sidhe. He fought to regain her by playing fidchell (chess) with Eochaid and eventually abducted Etain by seizing her and rising through the smoke-hole of Eochaid's hall in the form of *swans*. [13]

Miled (I) Ancestor of the *Milesians.* Grandson of *Bregon*. He sailed from Spain to avenge the death of his uncle (sometimes called brother), *Ith*. The *Tuatha de Danaan* caused Ireland to be swathed in a magic mist, so that he called the place 'Muic Inis' or Pig Island. He willed the land to his sons *Eber* and *Eremon*. [15]

Milesians (I) The sons of *Miled* and ancestors of the Gaels. They came to Ireland via Scythia, Egypt and Spain. They held the land after the departure of the *Tuatha de Danaan*. [15]

Mimir (N) God of the sea, which is sometimes named 'Mimir's well'. Its draughts gave him knowledge of all things past and future, and *Odin* traded one of his own eyes for a drink of it. Like the Celtic *Bran*, Mimir's head when cut off, became oracular and Odin preserved and consulted it long afterwards. Mimir is clearly a god of primeval power and qualities. In some versions of the Norse myths, *Yggdrasil*, the world-tree, is named Mimameid, Mimir's tree, after him. [53]

Minerva (RB) In Celtic understanding, the Goddess took many forms, but she was especially revealed as a goddess of wisdom, governing the inspired wisdom of the initiate. Minerva's chief temple in Britain was at Bath where she was twinned with the native goddess, *Sulis*. The veneration of the virgin goddess of wisdom and of war was already well-established in Britain: the attributes of Minerva are given to *Brigantia*. [59, 114]

Mochaomhog (I) The priest who cared for the enchanted children of *Lir*, *Fionnuala* and her brothers. He fashioned chains of silver for their necks, heard their story and instructed them in the Christian faith. He refused to give them up and eventually baptized them before they died, restored to their human shapes. [13]

Modron (W) Mother of *Mabon*. Her name merely means 'mother' and is a mystery title. No specific legend exists about her, although traces of her mythos are appreciable in the stories of *Rhiannon*, *Macha*, Demeter etc. She is the mother who loses her child. Her cult is closely tied in with that of her lost son, Mabon. Modron appears as the title of *Morgan* in a late sixteenth-century folk-story, where she is also called 'daughter of *Afallach*'. Her mythic lineage can be traced through *Morrighan* and is probably associated with the once widespread cult of the *Mothers*. She may be associated with Saint *Madrun*. [17, 28, 80]

Mog Ruith (I) 'Slave of the Wheel'. A druid or enchanter who lived on Valentia Island off south-west Munster. With his 'rowing wheel' — a prototype aircraft — he is supposed to have been a disciple of Simon Magus. His daughter *Tlachtga* was the only survivor of Simon Magus' ill-fated attempts to fly. His location, so near to the home of the *Cailleach Bheare*, suggests that he may have some connection with her cult. [99]

Mongan (I) King of Ireland. He was the son of Caintigerna who was visited by *Manannan* after her husband *Fiachna* had gone to fight in Scotland. Manannan promised to help her husband win his battle if she lay with him. Mongan was the son of this union. Manannan made her promise to allow Mongan to accompany him to the Other-world where he would be taught magical skills. Mongan was thus skilled in magic and poetry as well as kingship and overcame his enemies by the use of these arts. He was eventually killed in battle and passed into the Otherworld. Some consider him to have been a reincarnation of *Finn mac Cumhal* as well as an avatar of Manan-nan. In the Voyage of *Bran mac Febal*, Mongan's coming is likened to that of Christ. [99]

Mongfind (I) The jealous stepmother of *Niall*. She sent his mother, *Cairenn*, to serve her by drawing water from a well. Her four sons by Eochu the King of Ireland were passed over when Niall succeeded in winning all the tests to establish which of the boys had the right to the succession. [6]

Mor (I) Ancestress of the royal houses of Munster. A sun goddess whose throne is pointed out in the western seas of Ireland. [99]

Mordred (A) The son of *Arthur* and his half-sister, *Morgause*. This incestuous union made him both son and nephew of Arthur — anciently a powerful position according to the kingmaking rules of Celtic times which favoured the King's nephew, rather than his son as heir-apparent. (Hence the strong relationships which Arthur has with his other nephews, including more particularly, *Gawain*, whose family had greatest claim to the throne.)

In most versions of the Arthurian story, Mordred is depicted as a villain. His father sought to kill him when he realized that he had slept with Morgause; he ordered all children born at that time to be put into a boat and left to drown. Mordred escaped and was brought up with his half-brothers Gawain, *Gaheris, Agravaine* and

Gareth. In many versions he attempts to marry *Guinevere* when Arthur is on campaign elsewhere. He was finally slain by his father whom he mortally wounded at the Battle of *Camlan*. [20]

Morfessa (I) Great-knowledge, is the meaning of his name. He was the master of wisdom who dwelt in *Falias*, one of the four cities from which the *Tuatha de Danaan* came to Ireland. He gave the Stone of Fal into their care; this was the sacred inauguration stone which shrieked out under a rightful king. [5]

Morfran (W) The son of *Ceridwen* and *Tegid Foel*. His name means 'great *crow*'. He was also called 'Afagddu' or 'Utter Darkness'. He was so ugly that his mother sought to compensate this by the acquisition of great wisdom. It was for him that she prepared her *cauldron* of inspiration, but it was *Gwion/Taliesin* who drank it. Morfran was so ugly that, according to 'Culhwch and Olwen', he was not slain at the Battle of *Camlan* because his enemy thought him to be a devil. [17, 28, 80]

Morgan/Morgana le Fay (A) Daughter of *Gorlois of Cornwall* and *Igerna*, half-sister to King *Arthur*, mother of *Owain/Uwain* by *Uriens of Gore*. According to Malory, Morgan was 'put to school in a nunnery, where she learned great sorcery'. She becomes Arthur's most implacable enemy, attempting by means of magic to destroy him and the *Round Table* Fellowship. She was responsible for stealing the sword *Excalibur* and when this was recovered, succeeded in losing forever the scabbard which protected its wearer from all wounds.

To the writers of the medieval romances of Arthur, she was no more than a sorceress, yet behind her stands the figure of the ancient Celtic battle-goddess the *Morrighan*. Vestiges of this earlier identity remain embedded in the character as we now have it, such as her appearance with two other shadowy queens on the ship which takes Arthur to *Avalon* at the end of his days.

In Geoffrey of Monmouth's poem the 'Vita Merlini' she is described as ruling over a magical kingdom with her twelve sisters, while in later medieval romances such as 'Huon of Bordeaux' she has become Fata Morgana, the Queen of *Faery*, who steals away mortal men to be her lovers. In more recent times her name has become synonymous with witchcraft, although there are again signs that she is becoming restored as a more ancient and powerful figure more in accordance with her origins. She may also be identified with *Modron*, another aspect of the ancient Celtic Mother Goddess. [20, 29, 77, 80, 111, 124, 186]

Morgause (A) The second child of *Gorlois of Cornwall* and *Igerna*. She married King *Lot* of Orkney by whom she had *Gawain*, *Gaheris*, *Agravaine* and *Gareth*. Her fifth child, *Mordred*, was the result of her incestuous union with her half-brother, *Arthur*. She had a dark reputation, much like that of her sister, *Morgan le Fay*, and eventually perished at the hands of her own son Gaheris, who caught her in bed with *Lamorack*, son of the Orkney clan's greatest enemy, King *Pellinore*. [20]

Morholt/Morhold (A) The giant Irish champion who came every year to claim a tribute from King *Mark* of Cornwall. He was slain by *Tristan*, Mark's nephew, who received a poisoned wound from Morholt's sword. He was evidently of royal blood, being the uncle of *Isolt*. [20, 136]

Moriath (I) She was the daughter of *Scoriath*, King of Gaul; she was loved by *Labraid Longseach* while *Craiftine* played his harp, to make her parents sleep. [182]

Morrighan (I) The Great Queen. She was the archetypal form of the Goddess in Ireland, particularly associated with war (when she appeared in triple guise as *Macha, Nemainn* and *Badb*). She also combined with her bloodthirsty war-mongering, a lust for men — just like the Sumerian Inanna whom she much resembles. She fought on the side of the *Tuatha de Danaan* against the *Firbolgs* in the first Battle of Mag Tuired, after the second battle she foretold the end of the world, when moral virtues were ignored and where the land was laid waste. She offered her love to *CuChulainn* and after he rejected her, fought him in the shape of an eel and a wolf-bitch. Her normal appearance was in the shape of a battle-crow. She mated with the *Dagda* while straddling a river. Her name is really a title and is sometimes used as a collective noun for her three aspects — the Morrighan. There are obvious overlays with both *Modron* and *Morgan*. [5, 15, 27, 98, 103, 185]

The Mothers (Mamau/Matres) (C) Directly related to the great Neolithic goddesses of Europe, the triple mothers appeared all over the Celtic world, even becoming attached to certain Roman deities such as Mercury. The Romano-British *Matres* show the native influence combined with an intrinsic understanding of the classical Parcae (Fates). They are usually depicted as three seated, heavily draped women of mature years, bearing the fruits of the earth — cornucopias, fruit, barley-loaves, cakes, beer etc. Some also nurse babies (Dea Nutrix).

Their frequent depiction in reliefs denotes their universal function as guardians of the hearth, the land and of plenty. They are never given individual names but are addressed as the Mother of a particular locale — just as the Blessed Virgin *Mary* is entitled Our Lady of a particular place. While they undoubtedly flourished before Roman occupation, after it we find inscriptions addressing 'the Mothers of my Homeland' — of Gaul, Italy and Germany — showing their widespread understanding as the native goddesses or genia locus of every land. They were called the 'Mamau' in Welsh tradition. [59, 60, 103]

Muilearteach (S) The watery form of the *Cailleach Bheur*. She could appear as a hag or as a sea-serpent. On land, she would often appear to beg shelter at a mortal's fire, whereupon she would grow in size and ferocity. She had a blue-black face with one eye and raised winds and storms at sea.

Murine (I) Sister-in-law of *Lugh*. Mother of *Fionn*. She bore Fionn after his father's death and was unable to protect him, so she left him in fosterage with Bodhmall and Laith Luachra: a female druid and a woman warrior. [13]

Murias (I) One of the four cities from which the *Tuatha de Danaan* came to Ireland. Its master of wisdom was *Semias*, who entrusted the *cauldron* of knowledge to the *Dagda*. (See *Hallows*.) [5]

Muspellsheim (N) Realm of fire ruled by the fire-god, *Surtr*. The opposite of the ice-world of *Niflheim*: the combination of their heat and cold brought about the creation of the world.

Mylor (ST) He was a boy prince when his uncle killed his father. In order to block Mylor's becoming king, his uncle maimed him by cutting off his right hand and left foot, which were replaced by a silver and bronze appendage, respectively. These started to function as natural limbs and Mylor was subsequently executed in the monastery where he had taken shelter. This myth is parallel to that of *Nuadu*'s silver hand, and shows the persistence of the Celtic abhorrence for a *Wounded King*. Mylor's relics are kept at Amesbury Abbey and he is remembered on 1 October.

N

The Norns

Nanna (A) Goddess of flowers and vegetation. Wife of *Baldur*. When he was killed by *Hodur*, she died of a broken heart and went with him to *Hel*. When *Hermod* attempted to rescue Baldur, Nanna was asked to return with him. In the end, Baldur had to remain in Hel, and Nanna elected to stay with him. She sent a beautiful embroidery back with Hermod, as a token of her continued love for the world. [53]

Nantosuelta (C) Gaulish goddess, consort of *Sucellos*. She appears with a dove-cot or model-house on a pole and is accompanied by a *raven*. Her name means 'Winding River'. [103]

Naoisi (I) The lover of *Deirdriu*. She bound him on his honour to rescue her and flee from Ulster with her. He was slain by *Conchobar*'s client king, Eoghan. [12, 159]

Nasciens (A) The hermit dedicated to the service of the *Grail*. He appeared at various intervals in many of the medieval stories, as an adviser or explicator to the *Grail Knights* of the strange events and encounters made along their way. In earlier texts it is told how he was once a pagan lord named Seraphe, who took the name, Nasciens, at his conversion. Stricken blind when he tried to look within the Grail, he was healed by the *Grail Lance*. He came to Britain along with *Joseph of Arimathea* and lived on to become the hermit figure of later stories. [83]

Nechtan (I) He was the husband of *Boann*. The well of knowledge, over which nine hazel trees dropped their nuts was forbidden to any but he and his cup-bearers. Boann disobeyed him so that the well rose up and chased her, becoming the River Boyne.

Neit/Net (I) The male consort of *Nemainn*. His name may mean 'vigour' or 'exaltation in combat'. He is one of the primeval gods of Ireland and after his death at the second Battle of Mag Tuired, his sons divided the land between them. He was the grandfather of *Balor*. [185]

Nemainn (I) One of the aspects of the *Morrighan*.

Nemed (I) He came from Scythia into Ireland after the decease of *Partholon*. He beat the *Fomorians* in three battles but shortly afterwards died of plague along with 3,000 of his people. [15]

Nemetona (C) 'Goddess of the Sacred Grove' is the meaning of her name. Like many other Celtic deities, her name is a title, reverently hiding the local given name. She appears as the partner of *Mars* in his Romano-British guises. [103]

Nemhglan (I) He was the bird-like being who appeared to *Mess Buachalla* and made love to her. His son, *Conaire Mess Buachalla*, attempted to shoot at a flock of birds but Nemhglan flew down and laid a geise upon him to strip naked and proceed thus to Tara with only his sling-shot and one stone in his hand. By this method the druids recognized Conaire as the next High King.

Nentres of Garlot (A) One of the leading figures in the revolt of the eleven kings against *Arthur* at the beginning of his reign. He married Arthur's half-sister, *Elaine*, and eventually became Arthur's ally.

Neot (ST) (d. 877) Trained as a monk at *Glastonbury*, he became a hermit near Bodmin Moor at Neotstoke. He is said to have appeared to King *Alfred the Great* on the eve of the Battle of Ethandun. When Neot's oxen were stolen, he yoked stags to plough his fields. His feast-day is 31 July.

Nera (I) He was a servant of *Ailill*. One *Samhain* night, Ailill offered a prize to any who would go out and encircle the foot of a corpse hanging outside with a withy. It being the time of the dead, everyone refused but Nera. As he was about to perform the deed, the corpse asked for water: Nera carried him to a nearby house which was immediately circled by fire. At the next house, it became surrounded with water. At the third house the corpse drank three cups of water and spat out third upon the occupants who promptly died. Returning to claim his prize, Nera found the royal fort in flames and the King and his men beheaded. Nera descended to the underworld entrance of Cruachan to regain the heads and there lived with a bean-sidhe who explained that it had only been a vision and the best way to avoid it happening was to return to the royal fort and destroy the *sidhe* in which he now was. *Fergus mac Roigh* destroyed the place after plundering its treasuries for many wondrous *hallows*. Nera escaped with his sidhe-wife and child. [182]

Nerthus (N) The earliest name given to the Norse earth goddess. Tacitus gives an account of her image being carried in a flowered cart at spring festivals, at the end of which those who carried her were drowned along with the cart. In later tradition she became confused with *Freya*, who took over her original role. It is probable that the preserved, strangled bodies frequently discovered in bogland are relics of this sacrifice. [53]

Nessa (I) The wife of *Cathbad*. Her name had originally been Assa or 'Gentle'. But after Cathbad had killed all her tutors she took up arms as a woman warrior and was afterwards called 'Ungentle' or Niassa (Nessa). Cathbad surprised her bathing without her arms, but he spared her and granted her request to have only her as his wife. She bore *Conchobar* on the day prophesied as the birthday of Christ. [6]

Niall of the Nine Hostages (I) King of Tara in the late fourth century. He was the son of Eochu Muigmedon by *Cairenn*, a concubine, and was recognized by his father with his four step-brothers as a suitable heir to the throne. However, *Mongfind*, Eochu's wife, caused all the boys to be tested to see which would be king. She sent them to a prophetic smith, *Sithchean*, who set his forge on fire to see what implements the boys would rescue. Niall rescued the anvil and was accorded the winner. Mongfind set another test, dissatisfied that her children had been passed over. Sithchean sent the boys to fend for themselves in the forest, but they found themselves without water. Each boy went to a well which was guarded by a hag; she would only give water to the one who kissed her. Only Niall obliged her and she turned into a beautiful woman, naming herself as the *Sovereignty* of Ireland, which she accorded Niall. [6, 99]

Niamh (I) Daughter of *Manannan*. She loved *Oisin* and lured him into *Tir na Nog* where they lived together for 300 years until Oisin grew homesick. She gave him a horse to see his home once more, begging him not to set foot on the earth, but the girth slipped and Oisin fell with the weight of mortal years upon him. [13, 21]

Niamh (I) [2] The daughter of *Celtchair*. She married *Conganchas* in order to discover the secret of his invulnerability and how it might be overcome so that her father was able to kill him. [2]

Niflheim (N) Land of eternal cold which contained the nine infernal regions of Hel. Its icy fumes, combined with the heat of *Muspellsheim*, caused the creation of the world.

Nimue (A) The daughter of a vavasour, Dinas, with whom the goddess Diana would consort, because he was her god-son. *Merlin* saw her as a maiden making merry in the woods. She begged to be taught how to make a tower out of air. He succeeded and she imprisoned him, albeit willingly for love of her, in such a tower. According to Breton tradition this happened in the woods of *Broceliande*, in the Val Sans Retour, near the Fountain of Barenton, in Brittany. She is analogous, in some texts, to the *Lady of the Lake* and is sometimes called *Niniane* or *Vivienne*. The tradition of Merlin's imprisonment by this maiden probably stems from his withdrawal into the realms of *Faery* or the Celtic Otherworld which is frequently described in terms of a glass or spiral tower in which the poet or magician is imprisoned for a term in order to learn the mysteries of life and death. [20, 37]

Nine Worthies (L) According to medieval tradition the nine worthies were composed of three biblical heroes: Joshua, David and Judas Maccabaeus; three classical heroes: Hector, Alexander and Julius Caesar and three Christian heroes: Charlemagne, *Arthur* and Godfrey of Bouillon. These nine were evoked as epitomes of bravery and virtue and became enshrined in popular imagination only slightly below the saints themselves. [43]

Niniane (A) See *Nimue*.

Nissien (W) Brother of *Efnissien*. His name means 'peaceful', but he was unable to weave peace between his brother and those whom his brother insulted. [17, 80]

Njord/Niord (N) God of the sea and coastal waters who is in eternal strife with *Nerthus*. Originally of the *Vanir*, he later went to *Asgard* to join the *Aesir*. He married the ice giantess Skadi and they spent part of each year in each other's homes, personifying the division of the seasons.

Nodens (C) His chief sanctuary was at Lydney, Gloucestershire where the shrine had a guest house attached as well as a dormitory or 'abaton' for temple sleep. He is analogous to *Nuadu* and associated with Lludd Llaw Eraint (see *Llyr*) and *Gwynn ap Nudd*. No depictions of him exist, though his symbol seems to have been the *dog*, if the votive plaques found at his temple are any indication. He was a god of the waters, associated in Romano-Britain with Neptune. His chief native function was as god of healing. [28, 80, 121]

Norns (N) Triple-aspected goddess, or alternatively, three goddesses representing past, present and future. They ruled over man's fate and controlled his destiny, often negating each other's gifts so that little good seemed to come of them. The Saxons called them the *Wyrdes* and saw them as giantesses, or as giantess, elf and dwarf. Their like is to be found in most cultures, even controlling the fates of the gods. [1, 7, 53]

Nuadu (I) King of the *Tuatha de Danaan*. He lost his hand fighting against the *Firbolgs* and was thus disqualified from kingship (see *Sovereignty* and *Wounded King*). *Diancecht* and *Credne* made him a silver hand which caused Nuadu to be called Airgetlam (Silver-hand). However Diancecht's son, *Miach*, created a hand of flesh. He allowed *Lugh* to reign while he and his councillors conferred for a year on the best way to overcome the *Fomorians*, but he was killed in the second Battle of Mag Tuired. He is analogous with *Nodens*. [5, 15, 80, 121]

O

Odin's Ravens

Oberon (L) The king of *Faery*. The name seems to have been imported from the French story 'Huon of Bordeaux'. It is sometimes spelled Auberon and is believed to be associated with the dwarf Alberich of German tradition. [65]

Octriallach (I) He was a *Fomorian* who discovered how *Diancecht* had been able to bring the dead to life by means of the Well of Slaine. Octriallach showed his tribe the place and they filled in the spring. He was killed by *Ogma*. [182]

Odin/Votan/Wotan (N) Chief of the gods, all-wise, all-seeing, immutable. Son of the god Bor and a giantess named Bestla, he is usually portrayed as a one-eyed wanderer, wearing a cloak and wide-brimmed hat, and carying a staff which was really his spear Gungnir.

His desire for knowledge was endless, so that he even gave up one of his eyes for a draught from the fountain of *Mimir*, which conveyed all wisdom. He is said to have created men from two trees — the ash and the elm — and the earth itself from the body of the giant, *Ymir*. In *Valhalla*, the hall of the gods, he sat on his throne Valaskialf with two ravens, Hugin (Thought) and Munin (Memory) on either shoulder, and two wolves Geri and Freki at his feet. As god of war he watched over all battles, sending forth his warrior-maidens, the *Valkyries*, to summon the bravest warriors to his hall.

Unlike many gods, he was neither aloof nor vengeful, but was concerned with the nature of mankind, which he found at times both strange and laughable. In later time he was seen primarily as a magician and healer, but never lost his awe-inspiring qualities. He gained even further wisdom by hanging on *Yggdrasil* for nine days and nights during which time he learned the power of the runes. [53]

Odran (ST) (d. 563) He was one of *Columba's* companions in his exile on Iona. Legend tells that the monastery of Iona was hampered when the monks attempted to build the first church. Columba had a vision in which it was shown to him that devils were hindering the work and that the building would not remain standing unless a human victim was buried in the foundation. Odran offered himself and was buried alive in the foundations. After three days Columba dug him up. Odran was still alive and said: 'There is no wonder in death and Hell is not what it is reported to be.' Columba ordered the earth be replaced over Odran, saying: 'Earth, earth, on the mouth of Odran, that he may blab no more.' The cemetery was indeed called Rcilig Orain (Odran's Crypt). His feast-day is 27 October. [85]

Ogma (I) Warrior of the *Tuatha de Danaan*. He was the son of the *Dagda*, the husband of *Etain*, and father of *Tuirenn*. He was oppressed by *Bres* and the *Fomorians* whom he overcame in battle, as leader of the *Tuatha de Danaan*. He captured the speaking sword of the Fomorian King Tethra. He is credited with inventing the ogham alphabet which the Irish used in inscriptions, but not for writing. (The druidic prohibition on writing down knowledge persisted until very late in Ireland's history: its professional teachers, poets and judges all conned their art by heart.) Analogous to Gaulish god *Ogmios*. [59, 60, 103, 119]

Ogmios (C) A Gaulish god, analogous to *Ogma*. There is a native inscription to him as 'Ogmia' where he appears wielding the whip of the Invincible Sun and with his hair raying out in the manner of a sun-god. There are likely connections here with the native cults of *Maponus/Apollo*. [59, 103, 119]

Ogygia (G) An island, described by Plutarch as lying somewhere in the far west, whence heroes were shipped, to serve *Cronos* and learn many professional arts. It is analogous to the era called the Golden Age, only represented as a place rather than a time. Cronos was chained to the island by sleep, but his dreams dictated the actions of Zeus. [57]

Oimelc/Imbolc (C) The Celtic festival which was celebrated on 1 February. It was called also Feile Bhride, or *Brigit's* Feast. It marked

the lambing season and for this reason it is called 'sheep's milk' or
Oimelc. Sheep were under the protection of *Brigit*, who also sym-
bolized the coming spring. It is told in an obscure text how Brigit's
lamb fought against the *Cailleach*'s *dragon*, typifying winter, (see
Samhain). Scottish Gaelic regions still celebrate her feast in remembrance of a gentle mystery cycle about Brigit's imminent appearance,
while in Ireland, people make Bride's Crosses woven of rushes or
withies and in the shape of a three or four-armed cross. This custom
may derive from an earlier fire-ceremony in which this cross would
have been ignited and cast into the winter skies of February to hasten
the coming spring. The combat of Brigit with the Cailleach can still
be traced in some extant folk-stories. [186]

Oisin (I) The son of *Fionn* and *Sadbh*. He was the only hero, apart
from *Caoilte*, to survive the Battle of Gabhra, at which most of the
Fianna died. He was lured into *Tir na n'Og* by *Niamh* during the
battle where he intended to spend only a short time. However, many
hundreds of years passed and he longed for his home. Niamh gave
him a horse to go and see Ireland once more, telling him that he
must not touch the ground with his foot. The girth slipped and he
became an aged man. Saint *Patrick* attempted to baptize him, and
obtained from him the history of the Fianna so that it might be
recorded for later ages. Oisin was a bard: a tradition which enabled
James MacPherson (1736-96) to concoct a totally spurious set of Gaelic
Romances, supposedly collected from oral tradition, called 'Ossian'.
[13, 21]

Olwen (W) Daughter of *Yspaddaden* the Giant. She was the object
of *Culhwch*'s love and could not be won from her father without
her future husband fulfilling numerous impossible tasks. White
trefoils sprang up wherever she walked — accounting for her name
which means 'White Track'. Although she shares all the usual
attributes of a giant's daughter — courage, resourcefulness and beauty
— she does not enable Culhwch to fulfil his tasks in accordance with
most folk-stories. Whoever she weds will cause the death of her father:
and thus it happens, when Culhwch eventually wins her. [17, 28, 80]

Orc Triath (I) This *boar* was the possession of *Brigit*, the *Dagda's*
daughter. It is synonymous with *Twrch Trwyth*. One commentary
gives it as the name for a king, possibly indicating that the boar was
a kingly totem to aspire to.

Orfeo (L) The native form of Orpheus. In Scottish folk-story, Orfeo
goes in search of his queen, Isabel, and plays his pipes (or harp) to
good effect in the Underworld, thus releasing his lady. The same
story is told in a Middle-English text: Orpheo goes in search of
Meroudys or Herodis. The same story appears in native tradition in
the story of *Pwyll* and *Rhiannon*, and of *Midir* and *Etain*. [52, 94]

Orvandil/Earendel (N) The wandering seafarer who dwelt on the edge of the land of Jotunheim, where *Thor* was frequently a visitor. On one occasion Orvandil's toe had become frozen. Thor broke it off and threw it into the heavens where it became known as the constellation of Orion (Orvandil's Toe). The Anglo-Saxons called this Earendel.

Oscar/Osgar (I) The son of *Oisin*. He was killed by the High King of Ireland, whom he simultaneously killed. He had warning of his death from the *Washer at the Ford*. He was a reconciler of enemies but was fearless in battle. [13, 21]

Oswald (ST) (d.642) King of Northumbria. He became a Christian while in exile on Iona. When reinstated as king, after the death of Edwin the Usurper, Oswald gave Lindisfarne to Saint *Aidan*. He united Bernicia and Deira, but he was killed at the Battle of Maserfield. Aidan had once prayed that the king's generous hand never become corrupted. Indeed, his body was mutilated on the orders of pagan King Penda who ordered Oswald's head, arms and hands to be displayed on stakes. He was buried at Oswestry (Oswald's Tree) but his relics were scattered throughout Christendom — the hand remaining incorrupt. His feast-day is 5 October.

Otter (B) The otter is a strange magical animal whose genus totally baffled Celtic clerics who were always arguing whether it was flesh or fish and therefore edible during Lent. Anciently, the otter or water-dog was a transformatory beast. It is one of the guises which *Ceridwen* assumes when she chases *Taliesin*. In the many wonder-voyages or 'immrama' which *Maelduine*, *Brendan* and others take, they usually meet with a helpful otter who provides food for them or which performs this service for a hermit. Otter-skin bags also served as waterproof covering for harps in Ireland.

Owain (A) Historical hero, son of *Urien* of Rheged and *Modron* (*Morgan*). He fought on the side of the northern British against the Angles. He later became attached to the story of *Arthur* and is the hero of 'The Lady of the Fountain' and 'The Dream of Rhonabwy'. In the latter, he becomes the leader of a band known as the Ravens, who carry on a battle with Arthur's men while Owain and the king are playing chess. As his mother, Modron (analogous to *Morrighan*) often assumes the shape of a *raven* and promises to aid Urien and his family when they are in need in this shape, we can assume that the Ravens are not warriors, but in fact otherworld women in the form of ravens. In later medieval versions of his story, Owain became *Yvain* and features in Chrétien de Troyes' poem of that name: this substantially follows the story as set forth in the 'Mabinogion'. [17, 28, 80, 84]

Owen Glyndwr (W) Despite his close links with the English monarchy, Owen Glyndwr rebelled against Henry IV and started consolidating treaties with neighbouring barons which might well have set up a separate Welsh state if he had succeeded. A long drawn-out border-war swept the Marches of Wales and England. However, having shown himself a capable commander and man of foresight, Owen found his forces defeated, his family imprisoned and his hopes deferred. He remains one of the greatest of Welsh heroes who attempted to draw together the shattered links of British pride once more. He was credited with magical powers and, like *Arthur*, his death was obscure so as to give foundation to myths of his returning to aid the Cymru once again. [122]

Owl (B) The owl has been long considered to be a bird of ill-omen, especially if sighted during the day. *Blodeuwedd's* transformation into an owl, effected by *Gwydion*, is a punishment for having betrayed her husband, *Llew*; the story-teller comments that this is why owls bear the unlikely name of 'flower-face', which is the meaning of Blodeuwedd's name. In Scottish Gaelic, the owl is called '*cailleach*', or the old woman, and shows it to a bird under her protection. [18]

Oyster-Catcher (B) It is a bird under the protection of *Brigit* and is called Brid-eun, 'Bride's Bird' or Bigein-Bride, 'Bride's Boy', in Gaelic. [183]

P

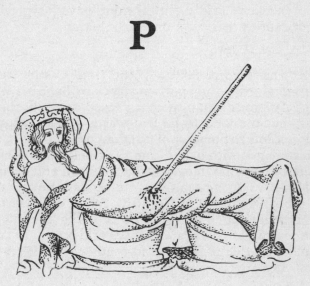

Pelles

Padern/Paternus (ST) (sixth century) The founder of Lanbadarn Fawr (Dyfed) where he was Abbot. When *Arthur* tried to steal the saint's tunic, according to legend, Padern caused the earth to swallow the king up to the neck. He was released only when he apologized. Padern's feast-day is 15 April. [72]

Palomides (A) The Saracen knight at *Arthur's* court who became one of the greatest *Round Table Knights*. Much of his career was spent in deadly rivalry for *Isolt of Ireland*, but he also took over the search for the *Questing Beast* after the death of *Pellinore*. He was made Duke of Provence by *Lancelot*. [20]

Partholon (I) Leader of the first invasion of Ireland. He was the chief of every craft; he cleared the plains for husbandry. His people were overcome by plague. He is the reaper of the last sheaf in modern Irish folklore. [15]

Patrick (ST) (c.391-461) Patron of Ireland. He was British by birth and was enslaved by Irish pirates who raided his home. He eventually escaped, having spent his captivity consolidating his spiritual life while tending his master's herds. He trained rather sketchily for priesthood and was determined to return to Ireland and evangelize its people. His success was doubtless based on preparatory work, already undertaken by anonymous monks already settled in Ireland, in addition to his assimilation of existing druidic and religious patterns, upon which he built. He put down the worship of *Crom Cruach*, is reputed to have expelled serpents from Ireland, and to have explained the Trinity theologically by means of the shamrock. His breastplate — or lorica prayer — in which the warrior through his prayer invokes Christ as his armour, is very typical of existing Celtic invocations. His feast-day is 17 March.

Pellam (A) See *Pelles*.

Pelles (A) The *Wounded King* of the *Grail* Castle. He received a wound through both thighs when struck by *Balin*'s spear: this was called the *Dolorous Blow*, since it caused not only the king to be wounded, but the land to be laid waste. His daughter, *Elaine of Corbenic* became the mother of *Galahad* by *Lancelot*. Galahad later healed his wounds with blood from the Grail. Pelles is one of several characters with similar names: *Pellam*, Pellean and *Pellinore*. These may indeed have once been the same person, the root of the name derives probably from the Cornish 'Peller' or wise man. Other scholars have identified him with *Pwyll* in the 'Mabinogion' and if true, this may well make him of otherworld origin. In later versions he became the father of Pellam and brother of Pellinore. (See *Fisher King*.) [24, 82, 83]

Pellinore (A) King of the Isles and one of the foremost knights of *Arthur*'s *Round Table*. His brother was said to be *Pelles*, the *Wounded King* of the *Grail* legends. His son was *Perceval*, in some versions. During the rebellion of the kings at the beginning of Arthur's reign, he killed *Lot* of Orkney, which caused a feud between the families. *Gawain* later killed Pellinore in an ambush, aided by his brothers. Until his death, Pellinore sought the *Questing Beast* which afterwards became the quarry of *Palomides*. [20]

Perceval/Perlesvaus/Peredur/Parzival (A) So various are the stories of Perceval that it is almost impossible to compile a straightforward history of his career. The earliest versions are the Welsh 'Peredur' and Chrétien de Troyes' 'Perceval' or 'Le Conte du Graal'. In these he was brought up by his mother, in seclusion from the world and especially from warfare and knighthood.

This rustic youth then encountered some of *Arthur's* knights and decided on such a career for himself, to his mother's despair. She gave him advice on how to conduct himself — all of which he applied in such an unworldly fashion as to leave a trail of havoc behind him. He behaved as the archetypal fool — a feature which led, in later versions, to his being called the 'Perfect or Pure Fool' and to authors associating his life and deeds with those of Christ.

After neglecting to ask the *Grail Question* and thus heal the *Wasteland*, he wandered having many adventures until he fell in love with a damsel. Love of her brought him to remembrance of who he really was and the real object of his quest — to find the *Grail* and ask the question. Much the same tale is told in the other stories: 'Perlesvaus', where he is the son of the king who has lost his lands ('perd les vals' — lost the vallies), is the most Christianized version in which Perlesvaus becomes a *Grail King* after the successful conclusion of his quest. This text has great depth and detail missing from the other versions.

In Wolfram von Eschenbach's 'Parzival', Parzival follows much the same train of events, and is incorporated as Grail guardian into the Templeisen or Knights of the Grail. In this story, the Grail family is seen as an esoteric blood-link, leading its members to serve the Grail in the world, according to their capacity: the men bear arms and the women bear children to the quest. There is a similar theme found within the story of *Amangons*. Wolfram incorporated many Eastern elements into the British original. As the 'Matter of Britain' became known and told throughout Europe so Perceval's role changed. His place as prime Grail winner was taken by *Galahad* in later versions. [2, 3, 17, 24, 26, 82, 83, 84]

Perilous Bed (A) The strange resting-place encountered by various of the *Grail* seekers. It appears as an ordinary bed, but anyone lying down on it is assaulted by invisible opponents who fling spears and by fierce beasts who attack the sleeper. *Gawain* successfully defeated the devices of the bed.

Perilous Seat (A) The Siege Perilous, so called because it swallowed up or cracked underneath whoever wrongfully sat in it. It was the place reserved at the *Round Table* for the *Grail Knight*. It was claimed by *Perceval* in the earlier versions of the story: he sat in it and it cracked apart while a disembodied voice warned him of his misdeed. He later caused the stone to reunite when he became a successful Grail Knight. In later versions, it is *Galahad's* place. It is said to represent the place of Christ at the table in the cenacle. [26]

Petrog (ST) (sixth century) He came from South Wales and founded a monastery at Wethinoc (Padstow) in Cornwall. He eventually became a hermit and is credited with having a great affinity for wild animals, especially a stag which he hid from huntsmen. His feast-day is 4 June.

Pig (B) The pig has a formidable reputation in Celtic lore. Whether it be the great *boar*, *Twrch Trwyth* or *Orc Triath*, or the pigs which *Pwyll* receives as a gift from the Underworld of *Annwn* by *Arawn*. Their appearance in the first and fourth branches of the 'Mabinogion', indicates an imbalance between the worlds and sure enough they cause war in Britain and their theft by *Gwydion*, is responsible for the slaying of Pwyll's son, *Pryderi*. There is a similar story in which *Arthur* and his men go to steal the pigs of *Mark*. The hero, *Culhwch*, whose name means pig-sty, was actually born in one because his insane mother was startled by pigs in the forest. It is he who is responsible for the slaying of Twrch Trwyth, the Great Boar himself. [18, 28, 80]

Potter Thompson (L) He found a secret tunnel running under Richmond Castle and discovered King *Arthur* and his knights asleep. A horn and sword stood by, but as he went to pick up the horn the knights began to stir. Terrified, he ran away hearing:

> 'Potter Thompson, Potter Thompson
> If thou hadst drawn the sword or blow the horn,
> Thou hadst been the luckiest man e'er born.'

Another story about the castle has a drummer boy sent down an underground passage to discover where it ran. He never emerged but his drumming is still heard. A similar story about finding King Arthur is found at Sewingshields. [98]

Prester John (A) Legendary Christian King of the East who, according to Wolfram von Eschenbach's 'Parzival', was the son of the *Grail* princess, Repanse de Joye and Feirefitz. He was also a known member of the Grail family and subsequent tradition makes him the Grail's guardian in the present age. [30]

Pridwen/Prydwen (A) The name of *Arthur's* ship in Welsh tradition, though Geoffrey of Monmouth calls it his shield. This confusion arose due to the similarity between shield and ship in the original latin. It is on Prydwen that Arthur sails to *Annwn* to recover the *Hallows*. [17, 28, 80]

Pryderi (W) Son of *Rhiannon* and *Pwyll*. He was snatched from his cot by a monstrous claw, causing his mother's ignominious servitude at the horse-block. Although not stated, the context of the story suggests an otherworldly foe, possibly the family of *Gwawl*, abducted him. He was found in a stable on May-Eve by *Teirnyon Turf Liant* who was guarding his mare which was in foal. The monstrous claw attempted to snatch her foal but was driven back by Teirnyon. Pryderi was called by his rescuer Gwri and brought up as Teirnyon's own son. However, on recognizing the likeness between the boy and Pwyll, Teirnyon returned the boy to his parents and so released Rhiannon from her bondage.

Pryderi later married *Cigfa* and succeeded to the Lordship of Dyfed. When the enchantments fell on his land, Pryderi and *Manawyddan*, his step-father, went hunting, and he was stuck to a golden bowl and trapped in the Otherworld. Manawyddan rescued him. In 'Math, Son of Mathonwy', Pryderi was robbed of his *pigs* by *Gwydion*, whom he followed and challenged to single combat. Gwydion exerted magic force and so Pryderi died. There are elements within this story which suggest that Pryderi is a form of *Mabon*, or that Mabon's lost mythos has been transmitted within the story of Pryderi. [17, 28, 80]

Pwca (W) Welsh form of Puck. He leads benighted travellers astray. Many versions of Pwca appear in British tradition, spelt variously as Pooka, Puck, Bwca, etc.

Pwyll (W) Lord of Dyfed. He encounted *Arawn*, Lord of *Annwn*, when out hunting and, in payment for an unintentional insult, offered to exchange places with him and fight his enemy, *Hafgan*. He spent a year in Arawn's shape and so won his friendship by good manners and successfully overcoming Hafgan, that he was given the title 'Lord of Annwn'. He won *Rhiannon* as his wife, but only after defeating her former suitor, *Gwawl*. They lived happily until the loss of *Pryderi*. [17, 28, 180]

Q

Questing Beast

Questing Beast (A) Also called the Beast Glatisant, this bizarre animal had a serpent's head, a leopard's body and *deer*'s hooves. As it ran, it emitted the sound of thirty pairs of hounds from its belly. In Malory, *Arthur* encounters it at a fountain soon after he is made king and *Merlin* explains it is endlessly pursued by *Pellinore*. After his death, it is pursued by *Palomides*. No explanation is given as to why the beast was sought in Malory, but in a French romance it is the offspring of a mortal woman who was subsequently torn apart by hounds. [20]

R

Round Table

Ragallach (I) He was a king of Connacut to whom it was prophesied that he would die at his daughter's hands. He ordered his wife to cast her into a bag and gave her to a swineherd to destroy. However, she was left at the door of a woman who raised her to become her own father's concubine.

Ragnarok (N) Literally, 'The Destruction of the Power'. The name given to the end of time when the gods (*Aesir*) and the *Frost Giants* will fight a last terrible battle in which the whole of creation will be involved. The most complete description of the end of things in Western mythology, Ragnarok was to be preceded by three terrible winters (Fimbulwinter) and three years in which man will become evermore self-destructive until he finally destroys himself. *Loki's* offspring, *Fenris* and *Hel*, will grow strong on this evil and finally break their bonds, stirring up the giants to attack *Asgard*. All will end in fire and death, though certain of the gods will go to dwell in Gimli, the highest heavens, while the evil ones are sent to Nastrond, the Norse equivalent of the Christian Hell. [1, 53]

Ragnell (A) The sister of *Gromer Somer Joure*, who enchanted her into the shape of a *Loathly Lady*. She helped *Gawain* find the answer to the riddle which Gromer set *Arthur*: 'What is it women most desire?' on the understanding that if the answer was correct, she would marry Gawain. They were married and on the wedding night Gawain discovered the true answer for, on kissing her, she became a beautiful woman. She said he could have her fair by night and ugly during the day, or ugly at night and fair by day. He could not decide and bade her to choose, thus realizing the answer to the question: 'women desire to have *sovereignty* or their own way.' The story also occurs as the Wife of Bath's tale in 'Canterbury Tales'. [14, 51]

Ran (N) Wife of *Aegir*. Goddess of storm and whirlpools. She dragged sailors down to their deaths in her terrible underwater kingdom. At one time, seafarers used to offer sacrifices to her and it was always considered wise to carry some gold to throw overboard in a storm.

Raven (B) The raven is one of the primal totems of the British Isles. In Ireland, it is the bird in whose shape *Morrighan* appears over battle-fields with her sisters, *Badbh* and *Nemainn*. Throughout Celtic and Arthurian literature, raven-women appear, performing much the same function as the Goddess. In one story, the 'Didot Perceval', *Morgan* herself appears as a raven. In Britain the raven is primarily the bird of *Bran the Blessed*, for 'bran' means raven. In that story he asks for his head to be cut off and buried at the White Mount, (modern Tower of London), to act as a palladium against invasion. This was done, but when *Arthur* became king, he dug up the head, not wishing any other to fulfil that task but himself. This act of hubris is perhaps represented in the tradition about the Tower's ravens who are supposed to similarly keep Britain free of invasion, and it is said that if they leave the Tower, Britain is doomed. It is for this reason that their wings are always kept well clipped. Ravens appear as the troops of *Owain*, in 'The Dream of Rhonabwy', while he and Arthur are playing a game of gwyddbwyll, a boardgame similar to the Irish bran-dubh (black-raven). They defeat Arthur's men, as Owain defeats Arthur in the game until the tables are turned. [18, 185, 186]

Rhiannon (W) Daughter of *Hefaidd Hen*, Lord of the Underworld. *Pwyll* saw her riding on a white mare and attempted to follow her, but she rode so fast that he was unable to catch her. He went to *Hefaidd*'s hall to beg her hand in marriage and was tricked into giving her away to her former suitor, *Gwawl*. Rhiannon showed Pwyll how to outwit Gwawl and they were married. Their only son, *Pryderi*, was snatched from the cradle by otherworld forces. While Rhiannon slept, the nurses and midwives killed some puppies and smeared her face with the blood, making believe she had killed and eaten her son, lest the blame should fall on them.

Rhiannon was set a penance: to stand at the mounting block and offer to take all visitors to the court upon her back, telling them her story of shame. She was relieved from this necessity on Pryderi's return. On Pwyll's death, she married *Manawyddan*. She followed Pryderi into an otherwordly castle where he stuck to a golden bowl. She likewise became stuck and suffered a long sojourn in the Otherworld with her son. She was released by the guile of Manawyddan.

The Birds of Rhiannon were said to be harbingers of otherworldly bliss: *Bran* and his company listened to them after his beheading, so that they were unaware of the passing of time. Rhiannon's attributes can be traced from the Celtic goddess *Epona* and the Greek goddess Despoina, daughter of Demeter Erynnes, but she is most closely modelled on the archetype of *Modron*, whose mythos she embodies. [17, 28, 80]

Rhydderch Hael (A) Also called Rhydderch the Generous or Rodarchus Largus, he was said to possess a magic *cauldron* which dispensed any amount of food to heroes. (See *Hallows*.) In the 'Vita Merlini', he appears as the defeater of *Merlin's* Lord, Gwenddolau at the Battle of Arfderydd. He may be an actual historical figure, Rhydderch ap Tudwal, who was king of Dumbarton in the sixth century. In the 'Vita', Rhydderch married Merlin's wife, *Guendolena*. [29, 111]

Rigantona (C) Great Queen - a title not a personal name. It is properly applied to *Rhiannon*, whose name may derive from this Celtic epithet. [103]

Rigru Roisclethan (I) Queen of Benn Edair — an otherworldly place. She was the mother of *Segda Saerlabraid* whom *Conn Cetchathach* sought to slay. She appeared just as her son was about to be killed at Tara in the guise of a wailing woman with a lowing *cow*. She is a clear form of *Sovereignty*. She warned Conn to put away *Becuma* or else Ireland would remain a *wasteland*. [6]

Robert the Bruce (1274 — 1329) Although he first swore fealty to Edward I of England, the Bruce soon followed in the footsteps of *William Wallace* in his defence of Scottish independence. After Wallace's execution, he was crowned Robert I at Scone. He was then temporarily defeated, and while exiled in Ireland he is said to have had his encounter with the spider, where he watched it try six times to fix its web to a beam. It was successful on the seventh attempt. The Bruce had also attempted to so secure his position six times and took heart. He finally won the treaty of independence as Scotland's sovereign in 1327, but died of leprosy two years later.

Robin Goodfellow (L) The son of *Oberon* and an earthly woman. He did the messages of *Faery* and passed into literary tradition with the help of Shakespeare and Jonson.

Robin Hood (L) The legendary outlaw who, with his band of merry men, roamed the forest of Sherwood robbing the rich to give to the poor. Such is the overlay of legend, that it is now almost impossible to state whether he was based on an actual person. Little John, Friar Tuck, Allen-a-Dale and Will Scarlet are all part of his band. Maid Marian lived with him in the wood, the pair of them becoming analogous in popular imagination with the Lord and Lady of *Faery*; they, with the rest of the band were favourite characters at fairs and disguisings. The later legends set Robin up as a form of surrogate king on behalf of Richard I, combating the evil Prince John and his henchman, the Sheriff of Nottingham. Robin met his death at the hands of the Prioress of Kirklees Abbey who gave him poison. [64, 94]

Roc (I) He was the steward of *Angus Og*. He had a son by the wife of Donn, father of *Diarmuid*, but Donn crushed it between his legs. Roc then struck the dead child with his wand, turning him into a *boar*, and from that moment the fortunes of Diarmuid and the boar were intertwined so that Diarmuid was given the geise never to hunt the boar. However, this is exactly what he did do, provoked by *Fionn*, and so met his death on its tusks.

Ron (A) Name of *Arthur's* lance.

Rosmerta (C) Her name means 'Good Purveyor'. She is a native goddess who was adopted into the Romano-British cult of *Mercury*, where she appears as his consort, adopting his caduceus and purse as well as retaining her own basket of fruit or *cauldron*/bucket of plenty. [60, 103]

Round Table (A) The institution of knighthood set up by *Arthur* at the behest of *Merlin*. The Table itself was gift a from *Leodegrance* of Cameliard, the father of *Guinevere*. It seated, according to various accounts, twenty-five, fifty or 150 knights, each of whom was dedicated to the service of the Round Table code of chivalry: right against wrong, good against evil. They met twice a year to exchange news of their adventures and details of outlaws, monsters and evil customs overcome. The Round Table esoterically symbolizes the coming together of peers, human and otherworldly, to watch over the fortunes of humanity. It is an encapsulation of the ancient concept of *Clas Myrddyn*. [20]

Ruadan (I) The son of *Bres* and *Brigit*. He fought on the *Fomorian* side in the second Battle of Mag Tuired and was sent to spy on the dispositions of the *Tuatha de Danaan*, particularly on their provision of arms and the nature of the healing well Slane with which *Diancecht* healed their men. He managed to wound *Goibniu* but the smith pierced him with the spear which he had been making. The similarities between this story and the accidental slaying of *Dylan* by *Gofannon* are striking. [6]

Ryons/Riance (A) Legendary king of North Wales whose curious custom was to trim his mantle with the beards of other kings he had conquered or slain. Not long after *Arthur* was crowned king, he received a message from Ryons demanding *his* beard to complete the border. Arthur replied that he was still rather young to sport a beard big enough, and proceeded to conquer Ryons instead. He seems to have been killed in a later battle with some rebellious lords.

S

Sheela na Gig

Sadbh (I) Mother of *Oisin*. She was enchanted into the form of a *deer* on refusing the love of Fear Doirche, but she found he had no power over her while she was within the dun of the *Fianna*. Bran and Sceolan, *Fionn's* hounds did not attempt to kill her when the Fianna found her out hunting. Fionn married her, but she left the protection of his house and was enchanted once more by Fear Doirche. After seven years, the hounds found a little boy, Oisin, Sadbh's son, who remembered his deer-mother. She was made to follow Fear Doirche and leave her son to the elements. [13]

Salmon (B) The salmon remains one of the symbols of great wisdom deeply embedded within Celtic mythology. As the salmon of knowledge it swam in the Well of Segais, imbibing the magical hazel-nuts which fell into its waters. It was prophesied that *Finegas* should catch and eat it, thus gaining all knowledge. However, it was roasted by *Fionn*, Finegas' apprentice. He burnt his thumb while turning it and so cooled it in his mouth and was the recipient of its power. This salmon was called Fintan. It was one of the shapes of *Tailiesin* in his escape from *Ceridwen*, and also the shape which *Tuan mac Carill* took. In the *Hawk* of the Achill story, the salmon was blinded by *hawk* on the coldest winter's night since the world began.[80]

Samhain (C) The Celtic festival which marked the New Year and was held on 1 November. Samhain eve was associated with the opening of the *Sidhes* and was a time of the dead. The feast marked the beginning of winter proper and its name may be related to 'summer's end'. At this time beasts were slaughtered for winter store and to conserve herds during the lean months; beasts were brought into winter pasture or into outbuildings. But most especially it was the inception of winter when the *Cailleach* ruled. In a curious early Irish text we hear of a strange boardgame which the boys of Rome play. At one end of the board is a cailleach with a *dragon* which she sends against a maiden with the lamb. The game was instituted by the sibyl, says the story, and explains why Samhain is so called. This contest is a clear remembrance of combat between winter and spring, which in Celtic terms were governed by the Cailleach and *Brigit* (the maiden with the lamb) respectively. (See *Oimelc*.) [186]

Samson (ST) (d.565) Bishop of Dol, Brittany. He was a Welshman who was trained by Saint *Illtyd*. He became a hermit on Caldy Island. One of the Scilly islands is named after him and it is on this spot that *Tristan* fought the *Morholt*. Like many other Celtic monks he was a great missionary. It is possible that he fled to Brittany due to the political unrest following the passing of *Arthur* at *Camlan*. His feast-day is 28 July.

Sarras (A) The holy city of the *Grail*, so named because it was once a city of Saracens (or alternatively, of Gypsies — the followers of Sara). Here the three *Grail Knights* came with the body of *Perceval*'s sister, *Dindrane*, and here *Galahad*, after looking within the Grail, died in an odour of sanctity and was buried within the great abbey. [24,83]

Scathach (I) Woman-warrior of Alba (Scotland), to whom *CuChulainn* went to be trained in arms. She was eventually bested by him and he was given her daughter, *Uathach* as his wife. Scathach is the eponymous goddess of Skye. She prophesied CuChulainn's fame as a hero.[5, 12]

Sceanbh (I) She was the wife of *Craiftine* the harper and was the cause of his helping to kill *Cormac* because she was his lover.

Scoriath (I) The King of Gaul whose daughter, *Moriath*, was beloved of *Labraid Longseach*. His harper, *Craiftine* played enchanting music which soothed him to sleep so that Labraid could sleep with Moriath. [182]

Seal (B) It was believed in Caithness that seals were fallen angels and certainly there are many stories in which they transform from seal to human. Like the *otter*, the seal was considered suitable 'fish' for consumption in Lent. Several families were supposed to be descended from seals and some had webbed hands or feet, a fairly common minor deformity. Some supposed seals to be the children of kings under enchantment, and certainly the tales of *selkies* show a marked tendency towards this tradition. They were called 'Cuilein Mairi' or 'Mary's Whelps' in Scots Gaelic. [183]

Seelie-Court (S) The Blessed Court of the *Fairies*. Like the *Aes Sidhe* of Ireland, they took their circuit around the boundaries of their realm at the major festivals of *Oimelc, Beltaine, Lughnasadh* and *Samhain*. They were normally beneficent in their dealings with mortals but were speedy avengers of insults to their kind.

Segda Saerlabraid (I) The son of *Rigru Roisclethan*. The otherwordly youth sought by *Conn* who required the blood of a boy of sinless parents to fructify the wasteland of Ireland. He gave unstinted affection to Conn and was even willing to die for his sake, but he was saved by his mother Rigru. [6, 99, 186]

Selkie (S) *Seal* people who have the ability to become human. They leave their seal-skins concealed and take human shape, or else a mortal man conceals the seal-skin and thus entraps a female selkie to live with him as his wife. When she finds her skin again she leaves her home and children, returning to the sea. In the ballad 'The Great Selkie of Sule Skerry' the selkie begets a child with a human woman and comes to claim his child, prophesying their certain death at the hands of her fisherman husband. Manannan makes a similar prophecy to *Bran mac Febal* about *Mongan*. [78, 94]

Semias (I) He was the master of wisdom who dwelt in *Murias*, one of the four cities from which the *Tuatha de Danaan* came to Ireland. He gave the *cauldron* of knowledge and satiety to the *Dagda*. (See *Hallows*.)

Setanta (I) The childhood name of *CuChulainn*.

Sheela na Gig/Sheila na Cioch (I) The image of the Sheela na Gig adorns walls and doorways of churches throughout Ireland. She is shown naked, with large breasts and holding her legs apart to reveal her vagina. She is one of the few actual depictions of Irish deities and represents the primal earth mother herself who gives birth and death. Her image was incorporated into churches to remind the faithful of their oldest allegiance. [62]

The Sidhe (I) The Hollow Hills wherein lived the *Aes Sidhe* or *Daoine Sidhe*, the Irish equivalent of the *Fairies*. The Sidhe is an otherworld abode whose entrances are natural land features and ancient burial mounds.[70, 55]

Sif (N) Wife of *Thor*, whose long golden hair was a byword. *Loki*, for a prank, cut it off while she slept, whereupon Thor demanded that he replace it. Loki went to the dwarves and found some who were so skilful that they could make real hair from gold. This led to the creation of other magical implements commissioned by the gods, including *Odin*'s spear, Gungrin, *Freya*'s magic ship and Thor's hammer, Mjollnir. [53]

Sigyn (N) *Loki's* wife, who despite his evil and mischievous nature, remained with him when he was imprisoned in a cavern beneath the earth. She caught most of the venom which dripped from the jaws of the serpent set to guard him, and thus prevented him from suffering as much as he ought. [53]

Silvanus (RB) This native Italian woodland god found a British counterpart already in situ. His name has not come down to us. Silvanus is sometimes surnamed Callirius (Woodland King) and is depicted with hammers, pots and billhook — the last the emblem of the native wood-warden. His beast seems to be the stag. (See *Cernunnos*.) [59]

Sithchean (I) He was the druid who, in the form of a smith, tested the sons of the King of Tara, to see which should be king. He tested them by setting his forge on fire to see what they would bear out from it. While four boys brought out various items still in the making, kindling, a barrel of ale and other items, *Niall* alone thought fit to bring out the blacksmith's tools — the hammer and anvil. In a further test, Sithchean sent them off into the forest as armed men for the first time to see how they would fare. In need of water, each boy came to a well guarded by a hideous hag who refused a drink until one of them kissed her. Only Niall complied and found himself embracing the goddess of *Sovereignty*, who declared him the rightful king.

Sleeping Lord (L) The many famous, legendary or heroic characters who are said to sleep under various hills in the British isles seem to have been a persistant tradition from *Cronos* to King *Arthur*. *Bran the Blessed* is also one of their number, while *Vortimer* is another. The tradition of an undying champion who sleeps beneath the land ready to wake in time of national danger may testify to an ancient concept of regnal sacrifice, by which the king would voluntarily agree to become the tribal representative in the Otherworld, thereafter being paid supreme honours and joining the ranks of the gods.[80]

Sluagh (S) The Host of the Dead who are seen fighting in the sky, the sound of which can be heard by mortals.[55]

Somerled (S) The Lord of the Isles and almost legendary ancestor of the Clan MacDonald, he was the product of Scandanavian, Gaelic and Pictish stock. He was responsible for driving out invading Norse

settlers in the Western Isles and restoring the predominance of the
Gael once more. His heraldic emblem of the black galley appears
in many coats of arms as the ancestral device of kings and princes.
He was born in about 1100 and was killed in 1164.

Sovereignty (C) The concept of the sovereignty-bestowing goddess
is especially marked among the Celtic peoples and their stories.
Originally Lady Sovereignty was called by the name of the land, e.g.
Eriu or *Logres*. Only the rightful kingly candidate could 'marry' her
in a symbolic union representing the king's obligation to the land
and its peoples; thus he was tested by having to encounter and
embrace Sovereignty who appeared as a loathsome hag. Her response
was to become her own beautiful self and announce his rightful
kingship to the people. The king who misused his power or who
became maimed or mutilated ruptured the mystic union with the
land and therefore with Sovereignty. The result of his continuing reign
was a wasting of the land - a theme central to the *Grail* legend. (See
Wasteland; Wounded King; Niall.) The Lady of Britain's Sovereignty
is *Brigit* or *Brigantia*, though *Britannia* has latterly assumed this
function. [80. 83. 98]

Speir-Bhean (I) The spirit or vision-woman encountered by poets
who wondered in lonely places. Poems about this kind of vision were
very common in the eighteenth century in Ireland, and were called
aislings. Very often the speir-bhean took on the form of the sorrowing
Ireland in search of a champion and the resultant poems from these
visions were a powerful and obscure means of promoting Irish
nationalism during this period. [186]

Spriggans (L) West Country sprites who act as the *Fairies*' bodyguard.
They have a reputation for frightening their victims whom they lead
astray and play tricks on.

Sreng (I) He was the *Firbolg* who was responsible for cutting off
Nuadu's hand, thus rendering him unfit for kingship.

Stoorworm (S) The Stoorworm is one of the great primeval water
monsters of British legend. Probably deriving mainly from the great
world-serpent Nidhoggi (see *Yggdrasil*), the Stoorworm was several
times larger than the usual monster. When it heaved itself out of the
waves the sea would engulf whole islands. Its appearance foretold
great devastation and it could only be propitiated by the sacrifice
of maidens. One king, in order to halt this barbarity and to avoid
his own daughter falling prey to it, promised her hand in marriage
and half his kingdom, as well as his ancestral sword, inherited from
Odin, to any man who could overcome it. *Assipattle* was successful
in thrusting burning peats into the beast's liver and its death agonies
caused it to vomit out its teeth which fell into the sea to form the

islands of Orkney, Shetland and Faroe, while its tail parted the land to form the Skaggerak between Norway and Sweden. Finally it curled itself into a ball and fell into the sea to form Iceland: its liver still burns and that accounts for the hot thermal waters and volcanic flames.

Sualtam (I) Husband of *Dechtire*. The mortal foster-father of *CuChulainn*. His severed head called warning to the men of Ulster when *Maeve* attacked them. *Bran's* head gave similar warning/protection to Britain.

Sucellos (C) 'The Good Striker', is the meaning of his name. He was a Gaulish god with a small following in Britain. He is shown carrying a long-handled hammer and frequently occurs with *Nantosuelta* (Winding River) as his consort. His function is uncertain.[59]

Suibhne Gelt (I) Seventh-century king of Ireland. Angered by the pealing of Saint Ronan's church bells, he threw the saint's psalter in the lake. He further angered the saint by killing one of his psalmists and Saint Ronan cursed him into madness. He imagined himself a bird and flew from tree-top to tree-top, roosting there at night. He entered into a contest with a hag, as to who could leap the furthest and broke the prison that he had been put in by concerned relatives. He was nourished by the milk that a swineherd's wife poured into the footprint of a *pig* and was slain by the swinehead who thought Suibhne was his wife's lover. He was confessed by Saint Moling before he died. This story is substantially the same as that of *Merlin*'s madness and is also associated with the legend of *Lailoken*. [61]

Sulis (C) Native goddess of the thermal waters at Bath who was twinned with *Minerva* at the Roman occupation. Her cult was evidently well-established since the Roman temple incorporated the worship of other deities apart from herself. Sulis was a goddess of the Underworld, of knowledge and prophecy. The story of how her temple came to be built is found in the legend of *Bladud* who, disfigured by a leprous skin-disease, rolled in the hot mud which *pigs* used to heal their own sores. He founded Sulis' temple over the spot. The healing waters of the hot springs still flow today, though there is some dispute as to whether they are suitable for use. The restored Roman temple is most impressive, incorporating all levels of building and indicating the vast spiritual resources available at that site [114]

Summer Country (A) A name for the otherworld kingdom ruled over by *Melwas*. He abducted *Guinevere* to this land and *Arthur* rescued her. It may be a source for the county of Somerset.

Surtr (N) The giant who ruled *Muspellsheim*, the realm of fire. He was always waiting for an opportunity to overwhelm the realm of the gods and it was believed that at the end of time, *Ragnarok*, he would set fire to the whole world.

Svart Alfar (N) See *Alfar*.

Swan (B) The swan has always had a mystical significance in Celtic mythology. Its skin and feathers were used to make the poet's tugen, a ceremonial cloak of his office, thus aligning the poetic function with 'the language of the birds', the secret formulas once more typical of the shaman. The children of *Lir* were transformed into swans by their step-mother and lived thus for hundreds of years until at last Saint *Mochaomhog*'s church bells released them.

Swithun (ST) (d.862) Bishop of Winchester. He was the tutor of King Ethelwulf who later made him Bishop. Swithun is popularly credited with control of the weather. He particularly asked to be buried outside Winchester Cathedral but was later transferred inside the church on 15 July; such was the heavy rainfall and accompanying miracles, that he was moved back to his original resting-place. If it rains on that day it is believed that rain will continue falling for another forty days.

Sword-Bridge (A) The bridge which separates this world and the Otherworld. It first makes its appearance in 'Culhwch and Olwen' where one of *Arthur's* allies, Osla Big-Knife, lays his knife down over a river in order to help Arthur and his host cross. It passed into the mythos of *Lancelot* who has to cross such a bridge to rescue *Guinevere* from *Melwas*. It also becomes one of the tests which the *Grail Knights* have to undergo in order to reach the Castle of the *Grail*. *CuChulainn* learns to cross a similar bridge when he is trained by *Scathach*. [17, 20, 23, 24, 82]

T

Tuatha de Dannan's retreat

Tailtiu (I) Foster-mother of *Lugh*. She was the daughter of the King of Spain who married *Eochaid* of the *Tuatha de Danaan*. She cleared a plain on the site of Coill Chuan, and that place was named Tailtiu after her. She was remembered ever after by mourning the games which were performed by Lugh and other kings after him. They were held for a month and became known as the Assembly of Lugh or *Lughnasadh* — after which the month of August is now called in Ireland.[99]

Taliesin (A) The greatest poet of the Island of Britain: he saw and foretold many of the events of *Arthur's* reign and the ages to follow. According to a seventeenth-century text (of admittedly earlier provenance) attached to the 'Mabinogion' collection, he was once named *Gwion* Bach and was set to watch over the *cauldron* of *Ceridwen* in which was brewed a drink of knowledge and inspiration intended for her son, *Morfran* or *Afagddu*. Some drops splashed out onto his fingers which he then thrust into his mouth, in order to cool them. So did he have access to all knowledge. He subsequently underwent a series of transformations (analogous to his poetic initiation) and was finally reborn of Ceridwen as Taliesin (Radiant Brow).

She set the baby poet in a coracle and he was found on May-Eve at the Salmon Weir by *Elphin* who became his patron. Taliesin subsequently rescued his master from prison and silenced the bards of *Maelgwn*. He sailed with Arthur on *Pridwen* when the king led the raid on *Annwn* in order to recover the *Hallows* of Britain. He has been identified with a sixth-century poet of the same name and is associated with both *Merlin* and Aneurin. A similar gaining of knowledge scenario is told of *Fionn*.

In Taliesin, the mantic and magical powers of the ancient poet-kind are revealed. His famous 'I have beens' boast, in which he lists the places and people he has been and met throughout time reveal the nature of his poetic initiation in which all knowledge is recapitulated. His pursuit by Ceridwen in her hag-aspect is a remnant of a once widespread myth in which the *Cailleach Bheare/Bheur* pursues her son, the God of Youth or *Mabon*, through countless transformations until he is possessed of all knowledge. [17, 28, 33, 76, 77, 80, 110, 111]

Tam Lin (S) The guardian of Carterhaugh Wood who exacted the maidenhead of any maiden who went there. His true love, Janet, rescued him from his bondage to the Queen of *Faery*. At Hallowe'en Janet dragged him off his *horse* and held onto him resolutely while he shape-shifted in her arms into various wild beasts. At last he was his own self and free of the Queen's spell. [52, 94]

Taranis (C) 'The Thunderer'. With his spoked wheel, he appears to have been a god of thunder. The Romans equated him with their god of the dead, Dis Pater, and with *Jupiter*. Taran is still the modern Welsh and Breton for 'thunder'.[103]

Tegid Foel (W) Husband of *Ceridwen*. His home is said to have been in Lake Tegid. He appears in many Welsh genealogies.[17]

Teyrnon Turf Liant (W) His epithet means 'Lord of the Raging Wave', but is generally believed to be drawn from the Celtic form 'Tigernonos' or Great Lord. He was the rescuer and foster-father of *Pryderi*. His part within the story of *Rhiannon* may once have been greater if the Celtic derivation of his name is any clue. Rhiannon marries *Manawyddan* who is closely associated with the sea and who might well share Teyrnon's title. Rhiannon is derived from the Celtic form, 'Rigantona' or 'Great Queen' — a suitable title for the wife of Tigernonos. The father of Pryderi is also uncertain, since Rhiannon was probably the wife of *Arawn* or a Lord of *Annwn* prior to *Pwyll*. [17, 80]

Thirteen Treasures of Britain (W) These are the sovereignty-bestowing objects, similar to the *Hallows*, which *Arthur* is said to have journeyed to *Annwn* in his ship Prydwen to fetch. The following list is a late medieval version from which we can yet discern their earlier prototypes.

1. Dyrnwyn, sword of *Rhydderch* the Generous: in the hands of a nobleman it would burst into flame from hilt to tip. (Arthur's sword *Caledfwlch* or *Excalibur* has the same ability in 'The Dream of Rhonabwy'.)

2. The Hamper of *Gwyddno Garanhir*: food for one man could be put into it and food for a hundred would be found when next opened. (This resembles the hamper which is stolen from the court of *Lludd*.)

3. The Horn of *Bran*: this dispensed whatever drink one wanted. (Bran the Blessed became known as a *Grail* guardian because of his *cauldron* of rebirth. This horn is clearly similar in function to the Grail which serves whatever food one likes best.)

4. The Chariot of Morgan the Wealthy: transported its owner wherever he wished to go quickly.

5. The Halter of Clyno Eiddyn which was attached to the owner's bedfoot by a staple: whatever *horse* one wished for would be found in the halter. (Such a dream-horse would be much desired by the horse-loving Celts.)

6. The Knife of Llawfronedd the Horseman: this would carve for twenty-four men at a meal.

7. The Cauldron of *Diwrnach* the Giant: would not boil a coward's food but only that of a brave man. (This is the one treasure mentioned in 'Culhwch and Olwen' which Arthur successfully fetches.)

8. The Whetstone of Tudwal Tudglyd: if a brave man sharpened his sword upon it it would draw out the life of any man it wounded, though a coward's sword would be unchanged.

9. The Coat of Padarn Red-Coat: it would only fit a nobleman, not a churl. (This resembles the Mantle of Faithful Wives which will cover the nakedness of a faithful woman but not an adulteress, in Arthurian legend.)

10. & 11. The Crock and Dish of Rhygenydd: in which would be found the food one liked best.

12. The Chessboard of Gwenddolau: the pieces were of silver, the board of gold and they played by themselves when it was set up. (This Chessboard appears in 'Peredur' where *Peredur* plays and, when his side loses, he casts the whole board into a lake). In that story it is termed 'the Chessboard of the Empress' where it clearly indicates the land of Lady *Sovereignty*.

13. The Mantle of Arthur: whoever wore it was invisible. (This cloak is also that worn by *Caswallawn* when he enchants Britain; it is probably also that of *Curoi mac Daire* who is specifically termed 'the grey man in the mantle'.) All thirteen treasures reveal a preoccupation with worthiness of the person finding or using them: they will not work for the unworthy. This is a clear indication of their function in the king's relationship with Sovereignty: they cannot be found

or wielded by any save the rightful king or champion of the king. They are said to be kept by *Merlin* in his glass house on Bardsey Island. [17, 28, 80, 186]

Thomas of Canterbury (ST) (1118—70) Archbishop and Chancellor of England under Henry II. His close friendship with the King did not survive his appointing Thomas Archbishop, for Thomas refused to prejudice the position of the Church by bringing its malefactors under secular law as Henry wished. He was exiled in France for six years but later returned to an uneasy peace.

When the King had his son, Prince Henry, crowned as his successor by bishops who had no right to this prerogative of Canterbury's, Thomas excommunicated the erring clerics. Henry then, enraged, asked his men to 'rid him of this turbulent priest'. Four barons readily despatched themselves for Canterbury, where they slew Thomas in his own cathedral. Henry did extravagant penance and Thomas became the centre of a great pilgrimage cult.

Thomas was not particularly saintly, though his defence of the Church's rights was impressive; as usual the success of his cult was dependent on his popularity with the people who like to ally themselves with a sinner turned saint against a choleric king. Canterbury was one of the richest pilgrim-centres in Europe until the Reformation. His feast-day is 29 December.

Thomas the Rhymer/True Thomas (S) Thomas of Ercledoune lived in the thirteenth century. He met with the Queen of Elfland and visited that country in her company. He was given clothes of the elvan green and given 'the tongue that cannot lie', i.e. the gift of prophecy. These prophecies were passed down and many were proven true. [52, 94]

Thor/Thunar (N) God of thunder and lightning. Possibly the oldest of the *Aesir*, he is known to have been worshipped over a wide area of the Northern world. 'Thor's Hammers' have been found in huge numbers, testifying to his popularity since these personal talismans were worn by his devotees. He was primarily the god of warriors: strong, hearty, free with women and interested in ordinary men, rather than noblemen, as was the case with *Odin*. His hall, Belskirnir, was the largest in *Asgard*. He was a great fighter of giants and was almost single-handedly successful in keeping the *Frost Giants* away from the realm of the gods. [53]

Tigernmas (I) He was an ancient, legendary king who instituted the worship of *Cromm Cruach*, which used human sacrifice in its rites. Tigernmas means 'Lord of Death'. He is credited with the introduction of gold-mining, silver-smithing and the weaving of tartans. [182]

Tigernonos (C) A Celtic title meaning 'Great King or Lord'. It is the male equivalent title to *Rigantona*, a title ascribed to *Rhiannon*.

Tintagil (A) The castle in Cornwall which has strong Arthurian associations. *Arthur* was conceived and born there, later *Merlin* took him from there to be raised by *Ector of the Forest Sauvage*. Although the present structure is of Norman origin, the site of a Celtic monastery lies adjacent on an island connected by a causeway to the mainland. This may well have been extant in Arthur's time. In earlier sources it is the castle of *Gorlois of Cornwall*, but later legends associate it with King *Mark* of Cornwall, although his real residence was probably Castle Dore.[20, 120]

Tir Na mBan (I) The Land of Women. The place of beautiful otherworld women, who welcome pilgrims and voyagers on the great voyages (immrama). Ruled over by its queen, the island provided a consort for every man, the best of entertainment, food and music. Both *Bran mac Febal* and *Maelduine* visited it. Time stood still, but both men found its timeless beauty too much for mortals and, though warned about its gifts of immortality, chose to sail away home.[19]

Tir Na mBeo (I) Land of the Living. The place of everlasting life.

Tir Na n'Og (I) Land of Youth or immortality where gods and men lived together in peace in a timeless world of beauty.

Tir Tairngire (I) Land of Promise. The place where all earthly dreams lay *in potentia* and where they could be fulfilled. A type of the earthly paradise.

Tlachtga (I) Daughter of *Mog Ruith*. She learned all his wisdom, travelling with him on his visits to the seats of magic throughout the world. She gave her name to the mound twelve miles from Tara where the druids kindled the fires of winter at *Samhain* (31 October). The legend which links her father with Simon Magus, makes her a kind of Sophia — the companion and assistant of Simon who acted as his pythoness.[99]

Tor (A) Believed to be the son of *Aries* the cowherd, Tor nevertheless desired knighthood — a rare enough desire in the breast of any humble born man in *Arthur*'s time. However it transpired that he was actually the natural son of King *Pellinore*, by the wife of Aries (before her marriage as *Merlin* pointed out). Thus it was proved, to the satisfaction of the medieval audience, that the natural blood of Tor's royal sire was bound to surface. He became a Knight of the *Round Table* and had many adventures. He was killed in the battle to free *Guinevere* from the stake.[20]

Trefuilngid Tre-Eochair (I) An ancient being who predated creation. He appeared to the assembly of Tara to tell it the history of Ireland.

He was of gigantic height and he controlled the rising and setting of the sun. He carried a stone tablet in one hand and a branch on which grew fruit, flowers and nuts concurrently. He inaugurated the office of historian for the first time. He was master of all wisdom. (See *Tuan mac Carill*.) [99]

Tristan (A) Nephew of King *Mark*. Son of King Meliodas and Queen Elizabeth of *Lyonesse*. He was called Tristan (Sorrow) because of the grief caused at his birth, since it killed his mother. After Lyonesse sank beneath the sea, he became attached first to the court of King Mark, where one of his first tasks was to kill the giant *Morholt*, and to fetch Mark's bride, *Isolt of Ireland*. But Isolt and Tristan drank a love-potion, made by Isolt's mother for the bridal pair, and were for ever afterwards snarled in a tragic love.

 After the affair became notorious, Tristan came to *Arthur*'s court, where he ranked second only to *Lancelot* in strength. From there he wandered to Britanny where he married *Iseult* of the Fair Hands. However, his love for Isolt of Ireland drew him back to her and he was eventually murdered by Mark and his henchman, *Andret*. Other versions tell of the episode of the black and white sails where Tristan, wounded and dying in Brittany, sent for Isolt of Ireland and awaited her coming with the show of a white sail. She came, but Iseult of Brittany, out of jealousy, told him that the sail was black. Whereupon he died and both women shortly followed him. Isolt died of a broken heart, Iseult of Brittany by her own hands, in remorse and sorrow. [20, 136]

Trow (N) Trows were inhabitants of the Shetlands. They lived in hills and are closely related to the Scandanavian troll. There are many stories about late travellers being 'trow-led'. To those who troubled to propitiate them, they proved trusty household spirits.

Troy (G) The enslaved inhabitants of Troy were rescued and led by *Brutus*, great-grandson of Aeneas, to Britain. Troy's legendary status as the origin of the British people has always figured importantly in the island's history. *Apollo*, one of the protectors of Troy, is found, in native form, in the guise of *Maponus/Mabon*. *Taliesin* may be considered to be a prophet of Troy's descendants since his poetic works tell of their likely fate in his inspired utterances before Maelgwn. [9, 17, 80]

Tuan mac Carill (I) The sole survivor of *Partholon's* party. He turned successively into a *deer*, a *boar*, an *eagle* and a *salmon*, in which form he was eaten by the wife of King Carill. He recalled the whole history of Ireland when the elders of Tara were attempting to chronicle its lands. He brought *Trefuilngid Tre-Eochair* to verify his story. (See *Fintan*.) [15]

Tuatha de Danaan (I) The people of *Danu*. They ruled Ireland after *Nemed*, and were descended from one of his great-grandsons. They were supposed to come from the northern isles of Greece where they had learned all the arts of magic. They brought four treasures with them from these parts: the Stone of Fal from *Falias*, which screamed under the foot of every rightful king; the Spear of *Lugh*, which came from *Gorias*; the sword of *Nuadu*, from *Findias*; and the *cauldron* of the *Dagda* from *Murias*. (See *Hallows*.) They fought long against the *Fomorians* and the *Firbolgs*, but were eventually vanquished by the *Milesians*, after which they retired to the Otherworld, *Tir na n'og* or the *Sidhe* or the Hollow Hills, as they are variously called.[15, 99]

Tuiren (I) *Muirne's* sister, *Fionn's* aunt. She married *Iollan*, one of the *Fianna* but he had a mistress in the *Sidhe*. Jealous of Tuiren, the woman turned her into a hound. While in this shape she bore twin cubs, Bran and Sceolan who became the hounds of Fionn; since they had human natures they could divine things which other dogs could not. She was changed back into a woman after Iollan promised the sidhe woman that he would love her alone.[13]

Tuirenn (I) Father of *Brian*, *Iuchar* and *Iucharba* who slew *Cian*,father of *Lugh*. He went to ask mercy for his sons and heal their wounds, but Lugh had hardened his heart. Tuirenn fell dead upon their bodies and they were buried together.[13]

Twrch Trwyth (W) The Great *boar* which is the object of the main impossible task *Culhwch* has to achieve. He was once a king, but was enchanted into the shape of a boar. With his seven piglets he terrorized the lands of Ireland and Britain, until he was driven into the sea by *Arthur*'s men. Culhwch's companions were able to steal the scissors, razor and comb which were kept between his ears. These items were ciphers for the more important quest for the *hallows* of Britain, on which Arthur was engaged. [17, 80]

Tylwyth Teg (W) The Fair Family — a euphemistic name for the *Fairies*. (See *Bendith y Mamau*.)

Tyr/Tiw (N) God of war. Most often called upon by warriors in battle. Together with *Odin* and *Thor*, one of the three principal deities, though he is usually called the son of Odin and *Frigga*. He helped bind *Fenris* until *Ragnarok* but when he put his hand into the wolf's mouth as a pledge it was bitten off. It is believed that he will fall in battle with *Hel*'s watchdog, Garm. [53]

U

The Star-dragon prophesying Uther's reign

Uathach (I) She was the daughter of *Scathach* and her name means 'spectre'. She let *CuChulainn* into her mother's military academy, but he slew her lover and was forced to take over his duties, of guarding the fort. Uathach became his mistress.

Ulfius (A) A knight who began in the service of *Uther Pendragon* and continued as *Arthur*'s chamberlain until his retirement. He assisted in *Merlin*'s plan to change Uther into the likeness of *Gorlois of Cornwall* so that he might lie with *Igraine* and beget Arthur. Together with *Brastias*, he is one of the earliest distinguishable figures in the Arthurian saga. [20]

Unseelie Court (S) The Unholy Court were, like the *svart-alfar*, a brand of faery-kind inimical to mortals. They are nearer in kind to the *Sluagh* and were quick to shoot both men and beasts with elf-shot from their bows.

Urban of the Black Thorn (A) In the 'Didot Perceval' he is the guardian of a certain ford to which *Perceval* comes and overthrows him. He is aided by several women in the shape of birds, and when Perceval kills one of them it regains its human form and is carried off by the rest to *Avalon*. There are references here both to the Irish battle goddess the *Morrighan*, who also took the shape of a bird, and to the *ravens* of *Owain ap Urien*, whose followers also had this ability. The common bird in all cases was the raven, which was sacred to the Celts. [26, 186]

Urien (A) King of the land of Gorre, he married *Morgan le Fay* and had by her a son named *Owain*. In older versions, he met *Modron* at a ford and lay with her. As she was the daughter of *Afallach*, King of the Otherworld and herself a shape-shifter, she promised to aid Urien and his family forever in the shape of a *raven*. This associates her closely with *Morrighan* — of which Morgan is derived. He parted from Morgan and became a supporter of *Arthur* and a *Round Table Knight*. He died while fighting with Arthur against *Mordred*. He has been identified with the sixth-century king of Rheged of the same name, who none the less lived much later than Arthur's supposed reign.[20, 26, 28, 33, 77, 80]

Uscias (I) The master of wisdom who dwelt in *Findias*, one of the four cities from which the *Tuatha de Danaan* came to Ireland. He gave *Nuadu* the Sword of Light from which no enemy came unwounded in combat. (See *Hallows*.) [57]

Usnach, the Sons of (I) *Naoisi*, *Ardan* and *Ainle*, who fled with *Deirdriu* to Alba.

Uther Pendragon (A) King of Britain. He fell in love with *Igraine*, wife of *Gorlois of Cornwall* and with the help of *Merlin*, who gave him the outward appearance of Gorlois, he visited Igraine and so was conceived *Arthur* who likewise took the name Pendragon (Chief Dragon) after his father's death. Uther died soon after his son's birth, leaving the kingdom in anarchy. He gave Arthur to Merlin to bring up secretly, since it was rumoured that the child might be that of Gorlois, as Uther married Igraine so precipitously after her husband's death. [20]

V

Vortigern's Tower

Valhalla (N) *Odin*'s great hall in *Asgard*, where he received the souls of dead warriors and entertained them with feasting and song. It had 840 doors, each wide enough for 800 warriors to pass though abreast. Its roof was of spears and its walls of shields. [1, 53]

Vali (N) God of light and spring. Son of *Odin* and the giantess Rinda. His sole purpose seems to have been to avenge the death of *Baldur*. However we do not possess any record of his killing of *Hodur*, accomplished it is said when he was but one night old. It is possible that this myth parallels that similarly lost story of *Mabon*. [53]

Valkyrie (N) The choosers of the slain who came to bear the bodies of worthy warriors to *Valhalla*. [53]

Vanaheim (N) See *Vanir*.

Vanir (N) The earliest of the Norse gods who later became attached to the *Aesir*, having begun in opposition to them. Probably they were fertility gods who became subsumed within later deities in much the same way that rival factions among the Greek deities exchanged places. Thus *Odin* or *Thor* succeed to earlier deities as did Zeus and *Apollo*. *Frey*, *Freya* and *Njord* were all Vanir originally, but came to be part of the incoming *Aesir*. Their original home was *Vanaheim*. [53, 162]

Ve (N) See *Vili*.

Vili (N) *Odin's* son and one of the creator gods, together with his brother *Ve*. They made the earth from the flesh and blood of the giant *Ymir* and the first human beings from the ash and elm trees. When Odin was once feared lost they assumed his place and duties until his return. [53]

Vivienne (A) Vivienne was the name given to the beguiling maiden in Tennyson's 'Morte d'Arthur': a portrayal far removed from the otherwordly nuances of earlier legend. (See *Nimue*.)

Vortigern (A) Usurping king of Britain who invited the Saxons as mercenaries against invading Picts and Scots and to fend off the waves of Saxon invaders who periodically encroached on British shores. The Saxon mercenaries soon became greedy for more and more lands and began inviting more of their own kind to join them. Vortigern attempted to arrange a peaceful meeting between the Saxons and Britons at Stonehenge, but the Saxons brought hidden weapons into the council and, at a signal, rose up and massacred the unarmed Britons. Vortigern was spared and fled to Wales where he attempted to build a tower — it would not stand however. *Merlin* Emrys explained that it was because of the warring *dragons*, one red and one white, which lay beneath the foundations. They represented the warring nations of Britons and Saxons. Vortigern fled again and was finally caught and killed by the rightful kings *Ambrosius* and *Uther Pendragon*. [9,105, 112]

W

Wayland's Smithy

Washer at the Ford (C) In both Irish and Scottish legend she is the otherworldly woman who represents the dark aspect of the Goddess. The warrior who encounters her washing bloody linen, may rightly suppose that his death on the battle-field is not far off. *Morgan* as *Modron* appears in this connection in a sixteenth-century folk-tale. *CuChulainn* saw two maidens washing his bloody garments on his way to his last battle. The Washer is also one of the guises of the *Morrighan*. [99, 103]

Wasteland (A) The country surrounding the Castle of the *Grail* which became waste when the *Grail King* was dealt the *Dolorous Blow*. This sapped his generative powers and severed the marriage bond which the king had with the land, represented by *Sovereignty*. At the end of the Grail quest, the *Wounded King* was healed and the Wasteland flowered once again. The Wasteland is often represented in the Grail cycle in the person of the *Loathly Lady*, *Cundrie* or Sovereignty in her hag-aspect — the ravaged face of the land before it shows again its fair face. [82, 83]

Wayland/Wieland (N) God of the smiths and smith of the gods. He was credited with making many of the great magical weapons and armour of the gods, including *Excalibur*. Like his prototype in Greek and Roman mythology, he was always depicted as a lame man, having been hamstrung by King Nidud, who stole one of his swords. Wayland exacted a terrible revenge on this mortal, luring his children to an island, killing the boy and raping the girl. Little now remains of his story, but he has assumed a role of great importance in British mythology as something of a tutelary spirit — not unlike *Herne* the hunter, another Anglo-Saxon deity. He is to be found associated with a number of ancient sites, including Wayland's Smithy in Wiltshire. [1, 41, 53]

Wild Edric (L) According to Walter Map, Edric lived in Shropshire and snatched an Elf-Maiden from the dance and married her, with the proviso that he was never to reproach her for her sisters' sake or the place where she had been abducted from. Needless to say he broke this proscription and she vanished. William the Conqueror is said to have desired to see the Elf-Maiden and befriended Edric. He is believed to be imprisoned in mines under the west Shropshire hills. When war breaks out he rides over the hills in the direction of the enemies' country. [32]

Wild Herdsman (W) This archetypal character appears in the person of *Custennin*, in the story of 'Culhwch and Olwen', but he is best seen in 'The Lady of the Fountain', where he appears as the guardian of the beasts of the forest. He is a black giant with a club, who beats upon the belly of a stag in order to call the beasts together. Traces of this archetype are perceivable in the earlier texts about *Merlin*, who is shown in the 'Vita Merlini' as riding on a stag. His function is the guardian of the totemic forces inhabiting the land; as genius of the primal forest and instructor in wisdom he presents a threatening but enlightening challenge to the questor. [17, 29, 80, 111]

Wild Hunt (L) The concept of the Wild Hunt — a spectral leader and his men, usually accompanied by baying hounds, who ride through the air or over the far hills — is common to many parts of the British Isles. In Glamorganshire the hunt is led by *Gwynn ap Nudd*. In southern England by *Herne* the hunter. The *Aes Sidhe* have a similar connotation in Ireland. The Saxons had the *Einherier*. The hounds are called *Gabriel Hounds* or Ratchets in Lancashire. [81]

William of Cloudesley (L) English outlaw who, like the Swiss hero William Tell, shot an apple off his son's head as well as 'many another marvel done for the amusement of poor folk'. (See *Adam Bell*.) [52]

William Wallace (1273 — 1305) He was one of Scotland's greatest heroes in their struggle for Scottish independence and was known as 'the Hammer and Scourge of England'. He was defeated by

Edward I at Falkirk and became a fugitive; during this time many legends are attributed to him including refusing the love of the Queen of England, and of fighting a lion in France. He was eventually betrayed and taken to London where he was tried, hanged, drawn and quartered. His work was completed by *Robert Bruce*.

Winefride/Gwenfrewi (ST) (seventh century) One of the principal saints of Wales. Caradoc, her suitor, on being refused by her, beheaded her; a fountain sprang where her head fell. Saint Beuno restored her life and she became Abbess at Holywell. The mineral waters of her shrine are still visited by people seeking miraculous cures. Her feast-day is 3 November.

Woodwose (L) The Wild Man of the Wood, sometimes also called Wooser or Ooser. In medieval times they were thought to inhabit the wild woods which then covered the land. They make frequent appearances in many forms of artwork from medieval times onwards, and were often used in masques to portray rustic or primitive folk. They were naked, clothed only in their hair. (See *Green Knight*, *Wild Herdsman* and *Jack in the Green*.)

Worms (L) *Dragons*. Worms abound in British folklore from Scotland down to the South, and from East Anglia to Ireland; many heroes have done battle with them. There is the *Lambton Worm* of Northumberland which ravaged the country and could join together if cut in two. *Kempe Owen* rescued his sister from being enchanted into the shape of a dragon. In Scotland the worms are usually of the seas' depths, living in deep lochs and swallowing victims. White Horse Hill in Wiltshire has a companion hill which is called Dragon's Hill — it is a good example of a land feature supposedly caused by the worm's frenzied writhing.[120]

Wounded King (A) The title sometimes given to the *Grail King* or *Fisher King* who received the *Dolorous Blow* through both thighs, robbing him of his kingly and generative powers. This tradition stems from early Celtic custom which forbade the rule of a blemished king, since this would reflect itself in the fertility of the land, causing it to become a *Wasteland*. The king was believed to have a contract with the land and was mystically married to *Sovereignty*. [82, 83]

Wren (B) The wren goes by the unlikely title of 'The King of the Birds' and the reason for this is given in an old story in which an *eagle* and a wren flew into the sky to see who could go highest. The eagle soon found himself alone in the air and was just congratulating himself when the wren, perching on his back, claimed the prize. Deeper than this is a primeval belief in the wren as the druids' sacred bird. In Ireland it was known as '*Fionn*'s doctor' and was hunted by the Wren Boys every Saint Stephen's Day where it was carried in procession with songs and shown to the people. It is seen to have been the bird representing the *Sleeping Lord* who, whether *Cronos*, *Bran* or *Arthur* must cede place, however great his reign. [183]

Wyrd (N) See *Norns*.

Y

Yggdrasil

Yggdrasil (N) The World Tree, a great ever-living ash which stretched from *Asgard* to *Hel* and bound together all the kingdoms of the *Aesir* and *Vanir*. It had three main roots, one in Asgard by Urd's fountain, the second in *Midgard* by Mimir's Well, and the third in *Niflheim* by the spring Hvergelmir. At the base of the tree the gods met daily to confer and pass judgement on mortals. At the top of Yggdrasil sat Vithofnir, the golden cockerel, who will crow on the dawning of *Ragnarok*. Other birds and animals who lived within the branches and roots of the great tree, include an *eagle*, a falcon, a goat and the squirrel, Ratatosk, and four stags: Dain, Dvalen, Duneyr and Durathor. At its foot lies the serpent Nidhoggi, gnawing at the roots. It will fall with the final battle of Ragnarok. [53]

Ymir (N) The first and oldest of the *Frost Giants*, formed from the frost of *Niflheim* and the fire of *Muspellsheim* nourished by the great cow, *Audhumla*; slain by *Odin* and his brothers *Vili* and *Ve*. They flung the body into *Ginnungagap* and from it formed the stuff of the worlds.

Yspaddaden Pencawr (W) In 'Culhwch and Olwen' he is the father of *Olwen* who sets *Culhwch* a number of impossible tasks before he will give up his daughter. He is wounded in the knee, stomach and eye by Culhwch and his companions, but cannot be killed until his daughter marries. He is the Welsh counterpart of *Balor*. [17, 80]

Yvain (A) See *Owain*. [3]

Bibliography

List A: Texts in Translation

1. *Norse Poetry*: W.H. Auden (Faber, London 1981).
2. *The High Book of the Grail*: Perlesvaus, ed. & trans. N. Bryant (D.S. Brewer, Cambridge 1978).
3. *Arthurian Romances*: Chrétien de Troyes, trans. W.W. Comfort (Dent, London 1963).
4. *Perceval: The Story of the Grail*: Chrétien de Troyes, trans. N. Bryant (D.S. Brewer, Cambridge 1982).
5. *Ancient Irish Tales*: T.P. Cross and C.H. Slover (Figgis, Dublin 1936).
6. *Cycles of the Kings*: M. Dillon (OUP/Geoffrey Cumberledge, London 1946).
7. *The Elder Edda*: trans. P.B. Taylor (Faber, London 1969).
8. *Fianagecht*: trans. K. Meyer (Figgis, Dublin 1910).
9. *History of the Kings of Britain*: Geoffrey of Monmouth, trans. L. Thorpe (Penguin, Harmondsworth 1966).
10. *A Journey through Wales*: Giraldus Cambrensis (Penguin, Harmondsworth 1978).
11. *The History and Topography of Ireland*: Giraldus Cambrensis

(Penguin, Harmondsworth 1982).

12. *CuChulain of Muirthemne*: Lady Gregory (Colin Smythe, Gerrards Cross 1973).

13. *Gods and Fighting Men*: Lady Gregory (Colin Smythe, Gerrards Cross 1976).

14. *The Knightly Tales of Sir Gawaine*: L.B. Hall (Nelson-Hall, Chicago 1976).

15. *Lebor Gabala Erenn* (The Book of Invasions): trans. R.A.S. MacAlister (Irish Texts Society, Dublin, 1938-56).

16. 'Vita Caradoci: Lifric of Llancarfan' in *The Lives of the Saints*: S. Baring-Gould (Grant, Edinburgh 1872).

17. *Mabinogion*: ed. Lady C. Guest (John Jones, Cardiff 1977).

18. *Mabinogion and Other Welsh Medieval Tales*: trans. P.K. Ford (Univ. of California Press 1977).

19. *Immran Brain: Bran's Journey to the Land of Women*: S. MacMathuna (Max Niemeyer Verlag, Tübingen 1985).

20. *Le Morte d'Arthur*: Sir Thomas Malory (Penguin, Harmondsworth 1981).

21. *The Silva Gadelica*: S.O'Grady (William and Norgate, London 1892).

22. *The Voyage of St Brendan*: J.J. O'Meira (Dolmen, Dublin 1976).

23. *Sir Lancelot of the Lake*: L.A. Paton (G. Routledge & Son Ltd, London 1928).

24. *The Quest for the Holy Grail*: trans. P. Matarasso (Penguin, Harmondsworth 1969).

25. *Sir Gawaine and the Green Knight*: trans J.R.R. Tolkien (Allen & Unwin 1975).

26. *The Romance of Perceval in Prose*: Didot Perceval, trans. D. Skeel (Univ. Washington Press, Seattle 1966).

27. *Tain Bo Cualigne*: trans T. Kinsella (Dolmen Press, Dublin 1970).

28. *Trioedd Ynys Prydein* (The Welsh Triads): trans. R. Bromwich (Univ. of Wales Press, Cardiff 1961).

29. *Vita Merlini*: ed. J.J. Parry (Univ. of Urbana, Illinois 1925).

30. *Parzival*: Wolfram von Eschenbach, trans. A.T. Hatto (Penguin, Harmondsworth 1980).

31. *Arthurian Chronicles*: Wace and Layamon, trans. E. Mason (Dent, London 1962).

32. *De Nugis Curialium*: Walter Map, ed. F. Tupper & M.B. Ogle (Chatto & Windus, London 1924).

33. *Welsh Poems: sixth century - 1600*: G. Williams (Faber, London 1973).

List B: General Bibliography

34. Anderson, W.: *Holy Places in the British Isles* (Ebury Press, London 1983).

35. Ashe, G.: *Camelot and the Vision of Albion* (Heinemann, London 1971).
36. Ashe, G.: *Kings and Queens of Early Britain* (Methuen, London 1982).
37. Aubert, O.L.: *Legendes Traditionelles de la Bretagne* (L. Aubert, Saint Brieuc Editions 1970).
38. Barker, D.: *Symbols of Sovereignty* (Westbridge Books, Newton Abbot 1979).
39. Blake, W.: *Poetry and Prose* (Nonesuch Press, London 1975).
40. Branston, B.: *Gods of the North* (Thames & Hudson, London 1980).
41. Branston, B.: *Lost Gods of England* (Thames & Hudson, London 1957).
42. Brennan, M.: *Stars and the Stones* (Thames & Hudson, London 1983).
43. Brewer's *Dictionary of Phrase and Fable* (Cassell, London 1959).
44. Briggs, K.: *Dictionary of Fairies* (Allen Lane, London 1976).
45. Bruce, J.D.: *Evolution of the Arthurian Romance* (Peter Smith, Gloucester 1958).
46. Butler, H.: *Ten Thousand Saints* (Wellbrook Press, Kilkenny 1972).
47. Carlyon, R.: *Guide to the Gods* (Heinemann, London 1981).
48. Carmichael, A.: *Carmina Gadelica* (Oliver & Boyd, Edinburgh, 1928-71).
49. Cavendish, R.: *Legends of the World* (Orbis, London 1982).
50. Chambers, A.: *Granuaile* (Wolfhound Press, Dublin 1983).
51. Chaucer, G.: *The Complete Works* (Oxford Univ. Press, Oxford 1912).
52. Child, F.J.: *The English and Scottish Popular Ballads* (Dover Publications, New York 1965).
53. Crossley Holland, : *Norse Myths* (A. Deutsch, London 1980).
54. De Jubainville, H. D'Arbois: *The Irish Mythological Cycle* (O'Donoghue & Co., Dublin 1903).
55. Evans-Wentz, W.Y. : *Fairy Faith in Celtic Countries* (Lemma Publications, New York 1973).
56. Every, G. : *Christian Mythology* (Hamlyn, London 1970).
57. Graves, R. : *Greek Myths* (Cassell, London 1958).
58. Graves, R. : *The White Goddess* (Faber, London 1948).
59. Green, M.J. : *The Gods of Roman Britain* (Shire Publications, Princes Risborough 1983).
60. Green, M. : *Gods of the Celts* (Alan Sutton, Gloucester 1986).
61. Heaney, S. : *Sweeney Astray* (Field Day Publications, Derry 1983).
62. Hickey, H. : *Images of Stone* (Blackstaff Press, Belfast 1976).
63. Hole, C. : *English Folk Heroes* (Batsford, London 1948).
64. Holt, J.C. : *Robin Hood* (Thames & Hudson, London 1982).

65. Hope-Moncrieffe, A. : *Romances and Legends of Chivalry* (Bell, New York 1978).
66. Humphries, E. : *The Taliesin Tradition* (Black Raven, London 1983).
67. Jobes, G. : *The Dictionary of Mythology Folklore and Symbols* (Scarecrow Press, New York 1961).
68. Jones, D. : *The Anathemata* (Faber, London 1952).
69. Karr, P.A. : *The King Arthur Companion* (Chaosium, Albany 1983).
70. Keightley, T. : *The Fairy Mythology* (Wildwood House, London 1981).
71. Kirk, R. : *The Secret Commonwealth* (D.S. Brewer, Cambridge 1976).
72. Korrel, P. : *An Arthurian Triangle* (Leiden E.J. Brill, 1984).
73. Lacy, N.J. : *The Arthurian Encyclopedia* (Garland, New York & London 1986).
74. Lindsay, J. : *Arthur and His Times* (Muller, London 1958).
75. Loomis, R.S. : *Arthurian Literature in the Middle Ages* (OUP, Oxford 1959).
76. Loomis, R.S. : *Celtic Myth and Arthurian Romance* (Columbia Univ. Press 1926).
77. Loomis, R.S. : *Wales and the Arthurian Tradition* (Cardiff Univ. Press 1956).
78. Mackenzie, D.A. : *Scottish Folk-Lore and Folk-Life* (Blackie, Edinburgh 1935).
79. Mangoel, A. & Guadalupe, G. : *The Dictionary of Imaginary Places* (Lester and Orpen Dennys, London 1980).
80. Matthews, C. : *Mabon and the Mysteries of Britain* (Arkana, London 1987).
81. Matthews, C. & J. : *The Western Way*, 2 vols. (Arkana, London 1985-6).
82. Matthews, J.: *The Grail: Quest for the Eternal* (Thames & Hudson, London 1981).
83. Matthews, J. & Green, M.: *The Grail Seeker's Companion* (Aquarian Press, Wellingborough 1986).
84. Matthews, J. &. Stewart, B.: *Warriors of Arthur* (Blandford, Poole 1987).
85. Merry, E.C.: *The Flaming Door* (Floris, Edinburgh 1983).
86. Moncrieffe I & Hicks, D.: *The Highland Clans* (Barrie and Rockcliff, London 1967).
87. Moorman, C. & R.: *An Arthurian Dictionary* (Univ. of Mississippi 1978).
88. Mottram, E.: *The Book of Herne* (Arrowspire Press, Colne 1982).
89. Murray, M.: *The Divine King in England* (Faber, London 1954).
90. O'Hogain, D.: *The Hero in Irish Folk History* (Gill & Macmillan, Dublin 1985).

91. O'Malley, B.B.: *A Pilgrim's Manual* (Paulinus Press, Marlborough 1985).

92. O'Rahilly, T.F.: *Early Irish History and Mythology* (Dublin Inst. of Advanced Studies, Dublin 1946).

93. O'Sullivan, S.: *Legends from Ireland* (Batsford, London 1977).

94. *Oxford Book of Ballads* (OUP, London 1969).

95. *Oxford Classical Dictionary* (OUP, 1970).

96. *Oxford Dictionary of Saints* (OUP, 1978).

97. Phillips, G.R.: *Brigantia*, (Routledge & Kegan Paul, London 1976).

98. Reader's Digest : *Folklore, Myths and Legends of Britain* (Reader's Digest, London 1973).

99. Rees, A. & B.: *Celtic Heritage* (Thames & Hudson, London 1961).

100. Reiss, E. & L.H. & Taylor, B.: *Arthurian Legend and Literature: an Annotated Bibliography. The Middle Ages* (Garland Publications, New York 1984).

101. Rhys, A.: *Arthurian Legend* (OUP, 1891).

102. Rhys, J.: *Celtic Folk-lore, Welsh and Manx* (Wildwood House, London 1980).

103. Ross, A.: *Pagan Celtic Britain* (Routledge & Kegan Paul, London 1967).

104. Scott, R.D.: *The Thumb of Knowledge* (Colorado Univ. Press, New York 1930).

105. Senior, M.: *Myths of Britain* (Orbis, London 1979).

106. Spence, L.: *History and Origins of Druidism* (Aquarian Press, London 1971).

107. Spence, L.: *History of Atlantis* (Rider, London 1930).

108. Spence, L.: *Minor Traditions of British Mythology* (Rider, London 1948).

109. Stark, E.: *St Endellion*, (Dyllansow Truran, Redruth 1983).

110. Stewart, R.J. (ed.): *The Book of Merlin* (Blandford Press, Poole 1987).

111. Stewart, R.J.: *The Mystic Life of Merlin* (Arkana, London 1986).

112. Stewart, R.J.: *The Prophecies of Merlin* (Arkana, London 1986).

113. Stewart, R.J.: *The Underworld Initiation* (Aquarian Press, Wellingborough 1985).

114. Stewart, R.J.: *The Waters of the Gap* (Bath City Council 1981).

115. Tatlock, J.S.P.: *The Legendary History of Britain* (Gordian, New York 1974).

116. Toulson, S.: *Celtic Journeys* (Hutchinson, London 1985).

117. Towill, E.S.: *The Saints of Scotland* (St Andrew Press, Edinburgh 1978).

118. Vince, J.: *Discovering Saints in Britain* (Shire Publications, Princes Risborough 1969).

119. Webster, G.: *The British Celts and their Gods under Rome*

(Batsford, London 1987).

120. Westwood, J.: *Albion: A Guide to Legendary Britain* (Granada, London 1985).

121. Wheeler, R.E.M.: *Report on the Excavations of the Prehistoric Roman and Post-Roman Site in Lydney Park, Glos.* (Soc. of Antiquaries, Oxford 1932).

122. Williams, G.: *When was Wales?* (Penguin, Harmondsworth 1985).

List C: Retellings, Fiction and Folk-Story

I. THE ARTHURIAN LEGEND AND DARK AGE BRITAIN

123. Anderson, P. &. K.: *The King of Ys* (Bael Books, New York 1986).

124. Bradley, M.Z.: *The Mists of Avalon* (Michael Joseph, London 1983).

125. Chapman, V.: *The Three Damosels* (Methuen, London 1978).

126. Herbert, K.: *Ghost in the Sunlight* (Bodley Head, London 1986).

127. Herbert, K.: *The Lady of the Fountain* (Bran's Head, Frome 1982).

128. Herbert, K.: *Queen of the Lightning* (Bodley Head, London 1984).

129. Houseman, C.: *The Life of Sir Aglovale de Gallis* (Methuen, London 1905).

130. Mockler, A.: *King Arthur and his Knights* (OUP, London 1984).

131. Powys, J.C.: *Porius* (Village Press, London 1974).

132. Steinbeck, J.: *The Acts of King Arthur and his Noble Knights* (Heinemann, London 1976).

133. Sutcliff, R.: *The Light Beyond the Forest* (Bodley Head, London 1979).

134. Sutcliff, R.: *The Road to Camlann* (Bodley Head, London 1981).

135. Sutcliff, R.: *The Sword and the Circle* (Bodley Head, London 1981).

136. Sutcliff, R.: *Tristan and Iseult* (Bodley Head, London 1971).

137. Treece, H.: *The Great Captains* (Bodley Head, London 1956).

138. White, T.H.: *The Once and Future King* (Collins, London 1952).

139. Yolen, J.: *Merlin's Book* (Ace Books, New York 1986).

II. FOLK TALES OF BRITAIN

140. Colwell, E.: *Round About and Long Ago — Tales from the English Counties* (Kestrel, Harmondsworth 1972).

141. Colwell, E.: *Tales from the Islands* (Kestrel, Harmondsworth 1975).

142. Marshall, S.: *Everyman's Book of English Folk Tales* (Dent, London 1981).

143. Picard, B.L.: *Tales of the British People* (Edmund Ward, London 1961).

144. Vansittart, P.: *The Dark Tower* (Macdonald, London 1965).

145. Vansittart, P.: *The Shadow Land* (Macdonald, London 1967).
146. Westwood, J.: *Tales and Legends* (Hart-Davis, London 1971).
147. Williams-Ellis, A.: *British Fairy Tales* (Blackie, London 1960).
148. Williams-Ellis, A.: *More British Fairy Tales* (Blackie, London 1960)

III. Irish Legends and Stories

149. Curtin, J.: *Hero Tales of Ireland* (Macmillan, London 1894).
150. Flint, K.C.: *Challenge of the Clans* (Bantam, New York 1986).
151. Flint, K.C.: *The Storm Shield* (Bantam, New York 1986).
152. Hazel, P.: *The Finnbranch* (Sphere, London 1986).
153. James, J.: *Not For All the Gold in Ireland* (Cassell, London 1968).
154. Lynch, P.: *Knights of God* (Puffin, Harmondsworth 1971).
155. Scott, M.: *A Bright Enchantment* (Sphere, London 1985).
156. Scott, M.: *A Golden Dream* (Sphere, London 1985).
157. Scott, M.: *A Silver Wish* (Sphere, London 1985).
158. Scott, M.: *Irish Folk and Fairy Tales*, 3 vols. (Sphere, London 1983).
159. Sutcliff, R.: *The High Deeds of Finn mac Cool* (Bodley Head, London 1967).
160. Sutcliff, R.: *The Hound of Ulster* (Bodley Head, London 1963).
161. Yeats, W.B.: *Fairy and Folk Tales of Ireland* (Colin Smythe, Gerrard's Cross 1973).

IV. Legends of the Northmen

162. Branston, B.: *Gods and Heroes from Viking Mythology* (Peter Loewe, London 1978).
163. Brown, G.M.: *Magnus* (Hogarth Press, London 1971).
164. Frith, N.: *The Spear of Mistletoe* (Routledge & Kegan Paul, London 1977).

V. Ancestral Stories — Tales from Prehistory

165. Caldecott, M.: *Guardians of the Tall Stories* (Arrow Books, London 1986).
166. Golding, W.: *The Inheritors* (Faber, London 1955).
167. Sutcliff, R.: *Sun Horse, Moon Horse* (Bodley Head, London 1977).
168. Sutcliff, R.: *Warrior Scarlet* (OUP, London 1958).
169. Treece, H.: *The Golden Strangers* (Bodley Head, London 1956).

VI. Stories of Scotland

170. Campbell, J.F.: *Popular Tales of the Western Highlands*, 4 vols. (Wildwood House, London 1983-4).
171. MacDougall, C.: *A Scent of Water* (The Molendinar Press, Glasgow 1975).

172. Manning-Sanders, R.: *Scottish Folk Tales* (Methuen, London 1976).

VII. WALES AND CELTIC BRITAIN

173. Ross, A.: *Druids, Gods and Heroes* (Peter Loewe, London 1986).
174. Walton, E.: *The Island of the Mighty Quartet* (Ballantyne, New York 1964-82).
175. Webb, H.: *Tales from Wales* (Dragon Books, London 1984).

VIII. MYTHIC BRITAIN – THE ENDURING PAST IN THE PRESENT

176. Ashe, G.: *The Finger and the Moon* (Heinemann, London 1973).
177. Cooper, S.: *The Dark is Rising Quintet* (Chatto & Windus, London 1965-77).
178. Garner, A.: *The Owl Service* (Collins, London 1967).
179. Haynes, B.: *The Moon Stallion* (Mirror Books, London 1978).
180. Kipling, R.: *Puck of Pook's Hill* (Macmillan, London 1983).
181. Lewis, C.S.: *That Hideous Strength* (Bodley Head, London 1945).

List D: Supplementary Titles

182. Ellis, P.B.: *A Dictionary of Irish Mythology* (Constable, London 1987).
183. Forbers, A.R.: *Gaelic Names of Beasts, Birds, Fish, Insects, Reptiles etc.* (Oliver & Boyd, Edinburgh 1905).
184. Keen. M.: *Outlaws of Medieval England* (Routledge & Kegan Paul, London 1961).
185. Le Roux, F.: & Guyonvarc'H, C.J. *Morrigan-Bodb-Macha* (Ogam-Celticum, Rennes 1983).
186. Matthews, C.: *Arthur and the Sovereignty of Britain: King and Goddess in the Mabinogion* (Arkana, London 1989).
187. Matthews, J.: *Boadicea* (Firebird Books, Poole 1988).
188. Matthews, J.: *Fionn mac Cumhal* (Firebird, Poole 1988).
189. Middleton, H.: *Son of Two Worlds* (Rider, London 1987).
190. Spence, L.: *Dictionary of Medieval Romance and Romance Writers* (G. Routledge, London 1913).
191. Stewart, R.J.: *CuChulainn* (Firebird, Poole 1988).

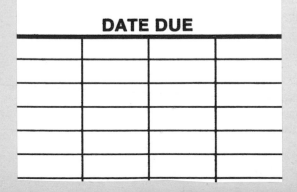